KENSINGTON M*

MW01122302

Collective Memory, Public History, and Toronto's Urban Landscape

Since the beginning of the twentieth century, Toronto's Kensington Market neighbourhood has been home to a multicultural mosaic of immigrant communities: Jewish, Portuguese, Chinese, South Asian, Caribbean, and many others. Despite repeated transformations, the neighbourhood has never lost its vibrant, close-knit character.

In *Kensington Market*, urban planner and public historian Na Li explores both the Market's dynamic history and the ways in which planners can access the intangible collective memory that helps define neighbourhoods like it around the world. Through examinations of Kensington landmarks such as the Kiev Synagogue, Hyman's Bookstore, and United Bakers Dairy Restaurant, Li traces the connections between the Market's built environment and the experiences of its inhabitants, past and present.

Using a culturally sensitive narrative approach that incorporates oral history and photographic records, *Kensington Market* is a must-read for those who have been drawn to this iconic Toronto neighbourhood, as well as anyone interested in the role heritage and collective memory play in urban planning.

NA LI is a research fellow at the Institute for Advanced Studies in Humanities and Social Sciences at Chongqing University and an adjunct professor at Shanghai Normal University, China.

NA LI

Kensington Market

Collective Memory, Public History, and Toronto's Urban Landscape

UNIVERSITY OF TORONTO PRESS
Toronto Buffalo London

© University of Toronto Press 2015
Toronto Buffalo London
www.utppublishing.com
Printed in the U.S.A.

ISBN 978-1-4426-4817-3 (cloth)
ISBN 978-1-4426-1621-9 (paper)

Printed on acid-free, 100% post-consumer recycled paper with vegetable-based inks.

Library and Archives Canada Cataloguing in Publication

Li, Na, 1977–, author
Kensington Market : collective memory, public history, and Toronto's urban landscape / Na Li.

Includes bibliographical references and index.
ISBN 978-1-4426-4817-3 (bound). – ISBN 978-1-4426-1621-9 (paperback)

1. Kensington Market (Toronto, Ont.) – History.   2. Ethnic neighborhoods – Ontario – Toronto – History.   3. Immigrants – Ontario – Toronto – History.   4. Collective memory – Ontario – Toronto.   5. Public history – Ontario – Toronto.   I. Title.

FC3097.52.L55 2015   971.3'541   C2015-901216-3

Unless stated otherwise all photographs were taken by the author.

University of Toronto Press acknowledges the financial assistance to its publishing program of the Canada Council for the Arts and the Ontario Arts Council, an agency of the Government of Ontario.

University of Toronto Press acknowledges the financial support of the Government of Canada through the Canada Book Fund for its publishing activities.

In gratitude to my parents, for their unfailing love and support; and to Liang Wang, who made all of this worthwhile

Contents

Illustrations

Tables

Preface

I would explore the back alleys, looking for vestiges of the texture of the historic city, largely composed of modest vernacular structures, sometimes abandoned, decayed, forgotten. These were the neighborhoods of the history of everyday life, testifying to our capacity to endow the built environment with grace and meaning. Sometimes such places were woven together organically in marvelous symphonies of urban form. But were they being saved?

– Anthony M. Tung, *Preserving the World's Great Cities:*
The Destruction and Renewal of the Historic Metropolis[1]

In 2002, I began seeking out surviving urban historical landscapes in the world's major cities. I wondered whether, if I compared preservation practices in different places, logics and patterns would emerge that would point to better alternatives than destroying urban areas for the sake of modern notions of progress.

My journey started in Rome, where historic preservation had become part of urban planning as that city's architectural values grew alongside powerful civilizations; I continued on to Paris, where sweeping vistas and architectural landmarks collided with *paysages des memoires*, then Amsterdam, where the affordable housing set an example for integrating urban preservation with social reform and public health. I then crossed the Atlantic and followed the historic Route 66 highway linking Chicago, in the heart of the industrial Midwest, to Los Angeles, "the land of milk and honey." The past along that highway was palpable in historic sites, monuments, trails, and buildings; these things expressed American popular culture in all its richness.

Since 2006, I have spent a lot of time in Toronto, where "half of the world" has settled by choice or circumstance.[2] I have lived here since 2008 and have thoroughly enjoyed being both an outsider and an insider. The city is now 176 years old and has accumulated a patina of time over the pastel shades where modernity and history converge in harmony. In this city my search for historical traces acquired a firm vernacular bent: I became fascinated by ordinary people's memories, stories, and aspirations, all of these embedded in the more nondescript buildings of a thriving cosmopolis. Their memories were like illuminations in old manuscripts, glowing brightly. Life in Toronto, now my second home, led me to Kensington Market, one of that city's oldest neighbourhoods. This book is about Kensington Market, its history, memories, struggles, aspirations, and changing landscapes.

Most studies of Kensington Market focus either on immigrant settlement patterns and cultural diversity, or on descriptions, inventories, and documentation of the architecture.[3] Few are dedicated to both, as this one will be. This book will also assume that no outsider can fully understand an insiders' sense of place. Robert Harney has observed that "ethnic neighborhoods can be studied as concentrated universes in two quite two different ways. One is accessible to plotting by analyzing factual sources, especially written by city records, and by forms of social scientific measurement. Another is more notional. It is about the mentalities of immigrants and about the psychic worlds they inhabit" (Harney and MHSO, 1985, 11). Unfortunately, few studies of such "psychic worlds" have been conducted. Some oral history interviews about Kensington Market were done in the 1980s, but these were poorly organized and rarely dealt with memories of living there. So this book addresses a community's psychological need to record and interpret its memories as part of Toronto's emotional terrain.

Chapter One, "Memory and History," starts with what is missing in today's debate about urban landscapes, highlighting three key concepts that will hold together ensuing discussions about Kensington Market: first, the multiple spatial dimensions of collective memory; second, how collective memory renders ethnic neighbourhoods contested; and third, communicative democracy – that is, how storytelling brings out the emotions embedded in urban landscapes. This chapter leads up to a fresh insight that relates to what I refer to as the culturally sensitive narrative approach (CSNA) to urban landscapes.

Chapter Two, "Kensington Market – an Urban Neighbourhood, a Cultural Metaphor," traces the historical evolution of Kensington Market.

It also examines the urban renewal planning efforts of the 1960s and concludes that their failure was actually a success for the Market's residents.

Chapter Three, "Collective Memory and Kensington Market," and Chapter Four, "From Sites of Memory to Memoryscape," take a selective look at sites of memory in Kensington Market. Richly narrated, those two chapters can serve as primary sources for the Market. The four sites they examine – Kiev Synagogue, the United Bakers Dairy Restaurant, Hyman's Bookstore, and the Market itself – were selected to represent different aspects of the Kensington landscape. These two chapters have benefited from the members of Kensington Market community with whom I worked between 2008 and 2010. They were exceedingly generous in sharing their stories and wisdom with me and helped me see the Market through their eyes. Many agreed to sit for interviews and walked me through their life journeys. During my fieldwork, they expressed a sincere interest in seeing this work in a book – this was, after all, *their* histories, *their* voices, and *their* memories.

Chapter Five, "A Sense of Time and a Sense of Place," summarizes CSNA and leaves readers with some questions to ponder. Many of the issues that have confronted Kensington Market in the past remain relevant today, in this time of urban preservation. This study demonstrates that CSNA is cross-disciplinary and culturally immersive but need not be expensive to conduct. It can serve as a phenomenology for refining theories about urban preservation studies for urban planners, preservation specialists, and public historians from the academic *and* professional worlds. Toronto is a city of diverse neighbourhoods that attracts immigrants from all over the world. This book, written from an immigrant's perspective, will also appeal to anyone with an interest in Toronto history, especially those who want to learn more about the city they cherish as their new home.

Cross-disciplinary work engages one's intellect *and* heart. "To snatch in a moment of courage, from the remorseless rush of time, a passing phase of life, is only the beginning of the task."

In Canada, the residents of Kensington Market were a huge source of wisdom and support. The Ontario Jewish Archives generously funded my fieldwork through the Dr Stephen Speisman bursary; also, the staff and friends at the Archives of Toronto, the Ontario Archives, the Ontario Heritage Trust, and Parks Canada, to name but a few, have contributed their professional advice and provided me with comprehensive documentation about Kensington Market. I owe a special thanks to Steven High, director of the Centre for Oral History and Digital Storytelling at Concordia University. Steve allowed me to work as a visiting oral historian at the centre, where I could process my interview data with *Stories Matter*.

In the United States, Richard Taupier, my doctoral adviser, funded my first two-year study at the University of Massachusetts–Amherst. Without his initial support and encouragement, I would never have come this far. My original theoretic framework grew out of the Advanced Planning Theory seminar I took with Elisabeth Hamin in 2007. She also provided perceptive comments that greatly improved my writing.

This is an interdisciplinary work, and faculty members of both the Department of Landscape Architecture and Regional Planning (LARP) and the Public History program within the Department of History at UMA have contributed to this work in many ways great and small. They include Mark Hamin, Patricia McGirr, Robert Ryan, Jack Ahern, David Glassberg, and Marla Miller. I have especially benefited from the advice and guidance of David Glassberg and Marla Miller, who carefully read the first draft and provided critical comments and astute editorial suggestions. David, as my true and far-sighted guide, encouraged me from our very first meeting back in 2007 to go farther down the path of public history. Marla taught me the value of the human factor in public history. I would not have been able to earn the Graduate Certificate in Public History without the gift of their time and wisdom.

An intellectual odyssey in North America can never be a solitary one. My travels have taught me a great truth – that if I open my eyes and heart, every place offers beauty and humanity. Anthony Tung's *Preserving the World's Great Cities: The Destruction and Renewal of the Historic Metropolis* launched me on my journey to Italy in 2002 and continued to accompany me to many historic cities in Asia. Six years later, in Tulsa, Oklahoma, we met at the National Trust for Historic Preservation conference. In my subsequent sojourns in New York City, Tony kept challenging my thinking about urban preservation. Equally important has been his insight and guidance, which I needed in order to finish writing this book.

The quality language training I received at Sichuan International Studies University, and the cross-cultural communication skills I learned at Shanghai International Studies University, prepared me early on to take up a complicated project like this.

I also want to thank all of the people whom I met on my travels for sharing their memories and experiences of place. They welcomed me into their lives and cultures, and each time I came back a richer person. My passion for vernacular architecture, for material symbols of local memories, matured during those precious encounters.

Friendship has been a large part of this work. My doctoral cohorts and friends from Amherst, Toronto, Montreal, and Ottawa provided tremendous logistical help in my field research and travels between Canada and the United States. Two individuals merit special mention. One is James Broens, my close friend from the Netherlands, who generously sponsored my Landscape Study Tour to France and the Netherlands in 2007. Jim has championed my study from the start. Another is Feng Dong, my friend from the Executive Program in Business Administration in Shanghai, who invited me to travel with him along Route 66 from Chicago to Los Angeles in the spring of 2009. This wonderful trip greatly expanded my critical understanding of historic landscapes and preservation in the United States; it also sparked my imagination when I came to write about urban landscape and memory.

Last, a lifelong passion for learning came before all of this. My parents gave me a heart to dream, the diligence to learn, and the perseverance to accomplish. They provided me with the best they had to transform my dream into a reality. For their unfailing love and support, I am deeply grateful. Liang Wang, my love, who always sees the best in me, accompanied me on many research trips in China, Canada, and the United States, and he made all of this worthwhile.

To all of these people go my thanks.

KENSINGTON MARKET

Collective Memory, Public History, and
Toronto's Urban Landscape

Chapter One

Memory and History: Urban Landscapes as Public History[1]

When it comes to history, the personal and experiential take precedence over the global and the abstract.

> – David Glassberg, *Sense of History:*
> *The Place of the Past in American Life*[2]

Collective Memory: Senses of Place

The meaning of a place evolves through negotiation with multiple layers, the deepest of which is collective memory. My interpretation of urban landscapes starts from this elementary concept. Collective memory acts as the meeting ground between the past and the present; it connects the physical world with a multitude of values – cultural, social, individual, and community; and through shared frames for understanding, it offers insights into the collective version of the past. Thus it is socially constructed. Maurice Halbwachs, in his pioneering study of *memoire collective,* writes that *cadres sociaux* – social frameworks – are indispensable to any act of remembering. He then merges two basic concepts of collective memory: it is the organic memory of the individual, which operates within the framework of a socio-cultural environment; and it is the shared version of the past created through interaction, communication, media, and institutions within small social groups as well as larger cultural communities.[3]

In this way, collective memory is different from the socially and culturally formed individual memory – or *collected* memory – that often engages in a dialogue with social psychology and neuroscience.[4] By constructing and sustaining the essence of urban places, collective memory can help us in very specific ways make intellectual and personal connections with urban landscapes. Meanwhile, as David Glassberg explains powerfully, the sense of history embedded in collective memory locates us in time and space, "connecting our personal experience and memories with those of a larger community, region, and nation." That is, a perspective on the past is at the core of what a community is and of the places its members care about.[5]

All collective memory involves a spatial dimension in a dynamic as powerful as the dialectic between remembering and forgetting. That mutually evolving dynamic can spark or inhibit collective imagination; to paraphrase Aby Warburg, objects and symbols are able to evoke memory and create cultural continuity,[6] harnessing the past to make a strong psychological statement about the present and future. This echoes Halbwachs and Coser, who write that "as soon as each person and each historical fact has permeated [this memory], it is transported into a teaching, a notion, or a symbol and takes on a meaning. It becomes an element of the society's system of ideas. This explains why traditions and present-day ideas can exist side by side."[7] Given there are different interpretations of the same past, however, the process can be fraught with politics, and it often involves emotional conflicts. This is why we deal with, not one single sense of place, but *senses of place*.

A small body of literature on urban planning and public history has examined how memory has shaped the urban physical environment. "Memory locates us as part of a family history, as part of a tribe or community, as a part of city-building and nation-making. Loss of memory is, basically, loss of identity."[8] In *The Power of Place*, Dolores Hayden explores place memory, writing that it "encapsulates the human ability to connect with both the built and natural environments that are entwined in the cultural landscapes."[9] And in *The City of Collective Memory*, Christine Boyer suggests that urban landscapes have the capacity to stimulate collective memory so as to evoke "a better reading of the history written across the surface and hidden in forgotten subterrains of the city."[10]

I will expand on these thoughts in Chapter Three. My point here is that individual reflection on seeing or experiencing a building generates a fairly weak form of memory; a stronger, culturally lasting memory requires us to experience and share *socially* the memory the built environment evokes in us. Cities and their architecture provide a collective set of memory "hotspots" that enable people to reproduce, recall, and retain their history through informal collective action and thereby create meaning. Buildings alone cannot preserve memory; the social practices attached to those buildings can do so.

As Kevin Lynch puts it so beautifully, "saving the past can be a way of learning for the future … Each celebration is also a nostalgic festival, which reaches back to memories of the dead kin mutually known to those who have met together. As we shall see, past and future time may be 'borrowed' to enlarge a present, just as we 'borrow' outside space to enlarge a small locality."[11] Envisioning the future with a sense of history connects the past, the present, and the future. That is why remembering, especially nostalgically, actually yearns for a different *place*, and a different *time* – as Svetlana Boym elaborates, the time of our childhood, the slower rhythms of our dreams.[12]

Multicultural Expansion

Besides having social and collective dimensions, memory is profoundly cultural. Aleida and Jan Assmann introduced the concept of *cultural memory* in the 1980s. Jan Assmann defined that term as comprising "that body of reusable texts, images, and rituals specific to each society in each epoch, whose cultivation serves to stabilize and convey that society's self-image."[13] Cultural memory, as a theory, does more than further complicate the idea of memory; as Astrid Erll points out, its central achievement has been to highlight how cultural memory, collective identity, and political legitimation all strengthen and rely on one another.[14] The most emotionally contested spaces are urban ones that have been drastically transformed by cultural diversity. The ethnic neighbourhoods in large North American cities, such as Boston, Chicago, New York, and Toronto, exemplify this conflict. What an outsider perceives as an enthralling ethnic urban landscape may, for an immigrant, be a social ghetto – a place of daily struggle and menial employment much like the Third World environment left behind.[15] What professional planners perceive as a seedy back alley to be cleared out may, for local residents, be a cherished place full of family and community memories. Until we expand the "official" narratives of those places, ethnic cultural voices will remain invisible and senses of places will be incomplete.

Displaced ethnic minorities, for example, reflect the power relations between those who control the city's image and those who have lost their identity and history. Note here the "qualitative difference between a collective memory that is based on forms of everyday interaction and communication and a collective memory that is more institutionalized and rests on ritual and media."[16] Luis Aponte-Pares convincingly demonstrates this power conflict in analysing how *casitas*, rooted in Puerto Rico, have been admired, scorned, celebrated, ignored, and destroyed – a process that reflects the displacement of the Puerto Rican population in New York City.[17] The ownership of space becomes a contested terrain: Whose history and whose memory are we, as preservation professionals, trying to preserve, at what cost, and for whom? Communities vary in the extent to which all of their members share a particular reading of history, since different versions of a community's history often coexist.[18] So urban memories are constantly evolving, defying any fixed historical reference point. If this fact is ignored, even the best-intentioned planning efforts may fail. Inviting individuals to express culturally distinct views, values, and visions can be a challenge, and balancing those things even more so.

A Culturally Sensitive Narrative Approach (CSNA)

More diverse and inclusive interpretations of history bring renewed attention to the ordinary and the vernacular. Interpreting and preserving the past often involves negotiating and renegotiating meanings and values through signs, symbols, artefacts, and landscapes, as well as engaging in political and power struggles. Sites of collective memory extend the temporal and spatial range of communication and are inevitably situational. I see this process as a personal and community journey, one that compels us to question long-held assumptions about cultural landscapes: Whose past and whose memory are we trying to interpret and preserve? Which version of history are we choosing to remember, or neglect?

This well-intentioned participatory process may come to grief when we are faced with local culture.[19] Some Asian cultural protocols,[20] for example, such as public respect for and obedience to the elder, the leader, or community gatekeepers, raise barriers to genuine public participation. Especially in these cases, emotional sensitivity based on understandings of the power structures and cultural norms within a particular community becomes critical. Even within the same general culture, members of the public arrive at planning tables with different agendas, cultural values, and personal priorities, and typically, these are different from what we, as professionals, have programmed. As Douglas W. Rigby observes, "the experience of many of the immigrant residents with the government of the old country had not prepared them for the form of participatory democracy on which neighbourhood involvement in planning is based."[21] So the challenge is twofold: to find ways to communicate and balance competing values through storytelling; and to do so in culturally diverse settings.

A culturally sensitive narrative approach to urban landscape addresses this challenge. This approach is based on shared authority over urban space: planners, including policy-makers and architectural designers, embrace a format of storytelling and oral history in order to elicit insiders' views, emotions, and, above all, collective memories of the place. Oral history as a methodology entails conducting life history interviews and analysing historical events; both deal with organic memory. Oral history provides fewer verifiable facts but does tell us about a community's psychology. I agree with Field, Meyer, and Swanson that "if you are trying to understand how and why people believe what they believe, think what they think, and – more crucially – why people act in ways they do, then memories and oral narratives or texts are of vital research significance."[22] Many cultures, especially those with strong oral traditions, rely on storytelling to pass on knowledge and share collective memory. In those circumstances, providing venues for storytelling may serve to highlight different histories and their connections to built forms that are most meaningful for different groups. In those venues, the planner needs to attend to how stories are told and emotions are evoked, through careful attention and critical listening.[23]

Oral history offers the most obvious academically tested means of engaging storytelling in the process. Scholars advocate using oral history in order to harvest collective experience from below[24] – that is, in order to include the collective experience of marginalized groups. Linda Shopes argues for essentially the same process – a reflective, critical approach to memory in the context of community history.[25] Dolores Hayden suggests applying socially inclusive urban landscape interpretations.[26] *All* scholars strive for more inclusive and participatory approaches to making the invisible visible. Tangible sources are often interpreted in overly specific ways; by contrast, oral history with its symbolic and intended meanings is *cumulative* across generations and is open to multiple interpretations. Preservation planners can gain insight from a focus on ordinary and vernacular understandings of the past. As Gerda Leneer points out, "by tracing one's personal roots and grounding one's identity in some collectivity with a shared past, one acquires stability and the basis for community."[27] To achieve this, we need to

Table 1.1. Comparison of Preservation Planning and Public History Perspectives

Explanatory factors	Convergent assumptions	Divergent foci	
		Preservation planning	Public history
Scope	Public → urban political process → historical and social power Collective experience: the past, present, and future Public participation and civic engagement	Future-oriented	Past-oriented
Authority	A shared authority vs a sole interpretive authority	Ownership of physical space	Historical interpretive power
Process	Communicative Narrative → emotional; cultural; psychic (memory)	Action-oriented → bounded rationality & Consensus driven	Interpretive focused → bounded rationality & multiple voices and perspectives
Historic Thinking & Analysis	The past is to be remembered → remembering vs. forgetting Representation & reconstruction → selective amnesia Context & frame of reference: locally defined	Visual & physical	Textual & historical

spend a great deal of time in the field, with humility and diligence, and allow residents to tell their own stories at their own pace and in their own terms.

Kensington Market, Toronto

In this study I address a prominent concern in urban preservation: how the intangible values of urban built environment are to be interpreted and preserved. A culturally diverse environment seems a good place to examine that question. This grand objective can be broken down into three more specific ones: to interpret the interactions among the social, cultural, and spatial logics that weave together the urban landscape;

to apply a culturally sensitive narrative approach as suggested earlier; and to delineate how planners could preserve and plan *with* public memories.

A historic survey of the field reveals three areas that have received inadequate attention. First, most studies utilize an "expert's" perspective to determine what *should* be preserved, developed, or demolished. Yet few of those studies ask what is *missing* from preserved urban landscapes. Many urban neighbourhoods took root and evolved without *any* planning. So it is important to examine these sites without heavily mediating them – that is, without distorting them by applying social and intellectual preconceptions about what they *should* be.[28] What government officials and planners deem historic may not always be what the public cares about.

Second, even with an increasing awareness of the social and cultural dimension of built environments, there has been fairly limited scholarly attention to what exactly makes landscapes political, emotional, and complex. When a certain version of history becomes the accepted narrative – and, eventually, the criterion for a successful preservation initiative – the simplified historic narrative excludes other interpretations.

Third, I concur with Randall Mason that "the preservation field is seen as having great responsibilities for managing the built environment and social memory."[29] However, understandings of the role of social or collective memory – an essential element, one that constitutes the intangible value in built environment – remain conceptual. There have been few in-depth studies of the reciprocal relationship between that intangible value and urban landscapes; there has been even less attention to connecting those sites of memory to tell a community story.

Why Kensington Market? In my early twenties, when I began travelling to learn about historic cities, I held a deep suspicion of anything official or touristy. I never felt obliged to include well-known sites on my itinerary – they were not my priority. Every time I visited such sites, which swarmed with tourists, I sensed I was actually travelling *away* from what was truly important. Always, I had an urge for something off the beaten path. I gradually learned that historic places *are* more mysterious than what tourists set out to find, so I set out to unearth those mysteries. When I found myself in Kensington Market during one of my frequent visits to Toronto, I instantly fell in love with every detail of that neighbourhood. Love is inarticulate; I would not want to put something that touches my emotions so deeply on the research agenda.

As the years passed, I found a Kensington Market that is less known to tourists – or to classically trained scholars. Most of the research on Kensington Market has focused on its cultural diversity, immigrant settlement patterns, or architectural inventory – all of which are legitimate subjects of study – but little of that research has tried to connect those three. Also relevant here is the whole frame of reference: an insider's sense of place cannot be fully understood by outsiders. So I followed my curiosity to Kensington insiders, directing my attention to *their* perspectives, emotions, memories, and sense of place. I started with a map of Kensington Market of the sort we planners use in our work, updating it every year for the sake of precision. My training pulled me towards planning minutes, city directories, census data, and historic records, and I diligently went through those, trying to piece them together to form a complete picture of Kensington Market. But those documents were bland, dimensionless, and utterly boring, as usual. Worse, in a strange way they smothered my inspiration. Something had to be missing here; Kensington Market, after all, had not been planned – it had just happened. Every time I walked its narrow, chaotic streets, I encountered something new. The cacophony of smells, flavours, colours, sounds, all excited me, and I found myself cultivating a whole garden of mysteriously inarticulate reasons to keep going back. All of this challenged me to rethink what I had taken for granted – which was refreshing. Where the map fails to tell, the imagination takes over. I kept wondering what exactly was missing from that map.

In a letter to the Historic Sites and Monuments Board of Canada (HSMBC) in 2003,[30] Carlos Teixeria, an urban geographer, proposed that Kensington Market be declared a National Historical Site. Based on his extensive research on community and neighbourhood change, ethnic entrepreneurship, and the social structure of Canadian cities, as well as two decades of field experience in various Toronto ethnic neighbourhoods, Dr Teixeira demonstrated how Kensington Market, a key reception area for immigrants to Toronto, remained remarkable: "the coming and going of its people – immigrants from all over the world – who have each contributed to the neighborhood and left culturally distinctive traces on its urban landscape. This area has played an integral role in the history of immigrant settlement in Toronto, and in Canada as a whole."[31] More important, this cultural tolerance and diversity was ongoing. At Dr Teixeira's urging, Kensington Market was designated a National Historic Site in 2006.

Two years later, on 25 May 2008, the HSMBC installed a plaque in the Market commemorating its historic significance. As the Honourable Jason Kenney, Secretary of State for Multiculturalism and Canadian Identity, was presenting it, he said: "Our government is proud to recognize Kensington Market as a National Historic Site. The commemoration of Kensington Market by the Government of Canada will ensure that the important history will be appreciated for generations to come."[32] However, given that the place evolved organically and that its businesses have thrived as a result of informal personal ties, "official" seems a strange word to apply to the Market.

For years, I have been travelling to different cities, trying to experience each as if it were my first and last encounter. I judge what I see with my own eyes. In John Steinbeck's words, "many a trip continues long after movement in time and space have ceased."[33] My owns ideas about what is historic and what is significant loosen up, and I become increasingly open to chance encounters, taking deep personal pleasure in signs of continuity and growth. My expectations fade, and I remember to approach each place with curiosity and humility. This book, then, is a journey of shared authority – between me, a committed preservation planner, and the community that has created Kensington Market over time.

Chapter Two

Kensington Market – an Urban Neighbourhood, a Cultural Metaphor

Kensington is an old part of the city. Its houses, many of them, were built in the 1870s and 1880s. The market that has given it a kind of fame is layered over with the struggles and hopes of a richly varied succession of immigrant groups ... Kensington has always had an interior life of its own. It has always been a home, a workplace, a village.

Jean Cochrane and Vincenzo
Pietropaolo, *Kensington*[1]

The residents are seeking an environment that is open to differences, where highly creative people are welcomed, regardless of ethnic background, creed, or sexual orientation. They prefer locations where there is an acceptance of multiplicity, where odd personal habits or extreme styles of dress are not only welcomed, but celebrated (Florida, 2002) ... Kensington is such a place, and is truly the village within.

Doug Taylor, *Kensington:
The Village Within*[2]

Land and History

In pre-European times, the Mississauga people inhabited the Toronto region. When the British arrived in the late 1700s, they took possession of it through a treaty signed in 1787 with three Mississauga chiefs.[3] The land under what in now Kensington Market was part of 156 acres of forest purchased by Colonel George Taylor Denison in 1815. Kensington grew out of what was an exclusively residential area. Russell Creek crossed what is now Bellevue Avenue; early on, it was covered over (and became part of Toronto's sewer system). Robert Denison, George's son, donated a large parcel of land at Bellevue and College.[4] The Denison family built a house they named "Belle Vue," to the north of what is now Denison Square; they also built the Church of St Stephen-in-the-Fields in 1858, the first church in Toronto west of Spadina Avenue.[5]

Before 1834, when Toronto was incorporated as a city, Kensington was a farming area just outside the city limits. With "a network of roads from the lakeshore into the hinterland, it became [a] wholesaling and distributing center."[6] With the coming of the railways in the 1850s, Toronto experienced rapid growth in manufacturing, wholesaling, and commerce. The railways were followed by the Toronto Street Railway (TSR), which after 1880 ran a horse-drawn streetcar service up Spadina Avenue and along College to Bathurst.[7] By 1884, streetcars were running along the area's northern and southern edges. Also by then, Toronto's central business district (CBD) was to the southeast.[8] South of the CBD, an industrial and warehousing zone had developed. Thus Kensington was located between working-class south Toronto (smaller lots, smaller houses) and wealthier north Toronto (larger lots, more expensive houses).

Around the same time, the Denisons began selling off parcels of their property around Kensington. When those lots proved to be too large and too expensive for the influx of British, Irish, and Scottish immigrants arriving in Toronto, the Denisons subdivided them. Those smaller subdivisions formed the basis of Kensington Market's later morphology as a tightly knit community.[9] Most of the Anglo-Saxon immigrants built single dwellings, duplexes, and rows of narrow two- and two-and-a-half-storey Queen Anne–style houses. This established the basic residential type in the Market. Many of today's street names reflect this early Anglo-Saxon influence (Figure 2.1).[10]

In the early 1900s, Toronto began to absorb its first non-British immigrants. Among the first arrivals were Jews from Central and Southern Europe. The Ward, an overcrowded immigrant reception area between Yonge Street and University Avenue,[11] would retain its Jewish character until the 1920s, when, as Michael Kluckner notes, "it became dominated by the next wave of poor immigrants – the Italians; west of Spadina, in the narrow streets lined with cheap houses, a European-style market area, a *shtetl*, grew up and was well established by the end of World War I." The 1920s were a time of liberalism, social change,

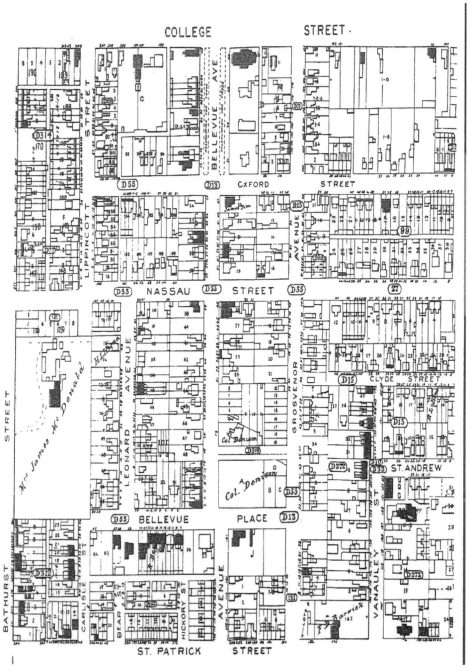

Figure 2.1.   Historic map of Kensington Market, 1884. Kensington Avenue, originally Vanauley Street; Augusta Avenue, originally Grosvenor Avenue; Baldwin Street, originally Clyde Street. Source: Goads Atlas, 1884.

NATIONAL ARCHIVES OF CANADA, PA-084814

Figure 2.2. The first Jewish merchants in Kensington Market were peddlers selling from carts and horse-drawn wagons, some of them rented. There were also stables and blacksmith shops in the area. Source: Library and Archives Canada, PA-84814.

and optimism; many Jews left the Ward and became landlords, renting their previous dwellings to poorer Jews. They began migrating into Kensington (Figure 2.2), drawn by the factories along Spadina Avenue south of Dundas Street and by the inexpensive housing and the prospect of setting up shops nearby. This shift towards the Kensington Market area marked a turning point for the city's Jewish community."[12]

City records show that the Jewish surge into Kensington Market, especially along Augusta Avenue, accelerated in the first half of the twentieth century. In 1901, Kensington Market had been 80 per cent Anglo-Canadian; by 1911, it was almost 100 per cent Jewish.[13] The reason why remains a mystery.[14] The City Directory for 1886 indicates that Kensington Market was home to quite a number of skilled artisans;[15] it was the Jews who arrived later who turned the Market into a commercial area.

A Street Market

Kensington market isn't romantic if it's your home... I detest Kensington Market... When we first came to Canada, my educated and merchant
father operated a grocery store on the south-west corner of Augusta and
Nassau, which now is part of the "picturesque" Kensington Market. We
barely eked out a "living," during the depression era. But it was the only
solution for us.

– Eda Shapiro, 1970

Kensington Market was now evolving into a mixed residential, commercial, and institutional area.[16] The influx of Jews selling from handcarts
changed the neighbourhood's character, transforming it into a street
market.[17] In the early twentieth century, most of the Eastern European
Jews coming to the area were refugees from Czarist pogroms or the
Bolshevik Revolution. Peddling wares by handcart was back-breaking
work, but their willingness to carry their goods to customers gave them
an edge over the shopkeepers.

The seductive call of the huckster, the discord of hand bells and motor
horns, the high-pitched wail of outraged housewives as they face the fact
of 60 cents for 11 quarts of cherries – sour ones too – the wrangle of half a
dozen determined females as they struggle to the death for that last lus-
cious watermelon, and, like the unceasing, rhythmic beat of the drum in
a Chinese drama, the steady quack of solemn ducks and the occasional
indignant outburst of an otherwise immaculately mannered hen – of such
is the merry din that breaks upon the visitor to the Thursday market in
Kensington Place."[18]

In 1926, an enterprising developer converted the ground floors of
a number of houses along Baldwin Street, between Kensington and
Augusta Avenues, into shops. These formed the nucleus for a concentration of shops and factories along Baldwin, Kensington, and
Augusta – the core of Kensington Market.[19] The city records show a
surge in development and renovation in the area between 1920 and
1935. After the Second World War, the Jews gradually moved north
out of the working-class Kensington Market towards Bathurst Street,
and new immigrants from other ethno-cultural communities started
to replace them.

A Multicultural Mosaic

Between 1945 and the early 1960s, about 2.7 million immigrants came to Canada, and one-quarter of them arrived in Toronto.[20] "Displaced persons of Eastern Europe and Italy, and disenfranchised Hungarian Jews escaping their homeland, made up a significant part of the post-war immigration to Kensington Market in the late 1940s and 1950s."[21] Some of them were war refugees – the Hungarians, for example, were escaping the Soviet invasion of their country in 1956.[22] The Portuguese also arrived in large numbers, in the 1950s, escaping the dictatorship in their home country. In 1953, "550 Portuguese men were recruited by Portuguese and Canadian authorities to fill a shortage of Canadian labour."[23]

Most of the Portuguese immigrants to Toronto chose to settle in Kensington Market, mainly because housing was affordable there and small business opportunities were available. Augusta Avenue came to be known as *A rua dos Portugueses,* or "the street of the Portuguese."[24] As the Portuguese took over the older Jewish businesses or started their own, Kensington Market became a multicultural gathering place for the city's new immigrants. In the mid-1960s, following the Jews, some Portuguese left the overcrowded Market and established neighbourhoods west of Bathurst Street, and the Portuguese influence declined. By then, however, they had transformed many of the buildings along Augusta Avenue and left a permanent mark on the Kensington streetscape.

In 1950s and 1960s, Kensington Market was transformed from a predominantly Jewish neighbourhood into a multicultural one. This was partly a result of 1962 amendments to the Immigration Act that put in place a more "colour-blind" approach to immigration. Immigrants now were entering Canada from almost every ethnic and cultural group in the world: Ukrainians, Poles, Afro-Caribbeans, Chinese and East Asians, and East Indians, among others.

Between 1961 and 1971, Kensington Market's population fell from 5,494 to 4,885; of those remaining, 3,280 were born outside Canada. Over the same decade, the area's ethnic composition changed dramatically: a decrease in European residents was accompanied by a sharp increase in Asian residents, from 100 to 605.[25] In the 1980s, this pattern continued. In 1986, 300 more area residents spoke Chinese as their first language than spoke English.[26] A decade later, the Chinese were the largest ethnic group in Kensington Market, followed by Portuguese, South Asians, Ukrainians, Jamaicans, and Filipinos.

Kensington Market's cosmopolitanism reflects that of Toronto more generally. The city's recent social history has been a reflection of Canada's immigration policy since the Second World War, when Toronto began to transform itself from "a comfortable but stodgy outpost of Anglo-Celtic hegemony" to a place that "holds the promise and fascination in lands of emigration."[27] Robert Harney, who has investigated this celebrated cosmopolitanism, argues that a city that relies on immigrants alone for its cosmopolitanism runs a number of risks. There is the danger that the resulting variety will be transient, that although the newcomers' ways will be tolerated for a time, afterwards yawns a hungry melting pot. Also, an "interesting" neighbourhood for the city walker may eventually evolve into a ghetto for those who live there, a place where the housing is substandard and the available work is menial.

Urban Renewal Planning in the 1960s

Kensington Market has been a staging area for immigrants since the first European Jews arrived in the early twentieth century. It has grown out of the daily needs of a multitude of immigrant groups, and it has acquired its colours and flavours through the hearts and labour of the new Canadians living there. This non-deliberate place-making is at the very core of the neighbourhood's character and is what makes the Market authentic despite the lack of architectural design or official plans.

Kensington as a community has changed over time, and this has led to various human and land use problems – traffic congestion, inadequate parking, and cluttered backyards, for example. The newly arrived immigrants have needed to find jobs and places to live while they adjust to their new social, political, and cultural milieu. In the 1960s, a series of pivotal events transformed Kensington Market: the Spadina Expressway project (eventually cancelled), the Urban Renewal Program, and the expansion of institutional land use in the area.[28] Some of those events would spill over into the 1970s and 1980s. Those forces represented conflicting interests that might have altered or commercialized, preserved or demolished Kensington Market.

In April 1961, Toronto's Public Works Committee asked various city departments concerned with development, health, and safety to prepare a report on the feasibility of creating a plan for Kensington Market. The committee stated that the main objective of any plan for the area should be to preserve and enhance the ambience of a street market.[29]

Kensington Market became one of six areas in downtown Toronto slated for urban renewal.

In Canada, the term "urban renewal" was first formally used in 1964 in amendments to the National Housing Act of 1944. This legislative change promised to improve neighbourhoods by providing the widest possible spectrum of opportunities for development. "The major feature of the new approach ... was the broad opportunity provided to utilize every technique and to examine a variety of approaches to the improvement of old neighbourhoods in downtown areas threatened by what was traditionally called 'blight' and 'slum.'"[30]

But the seeds of urban renewal had been planted much earlier, in the 1930s, with calls for slum clearance. With its justification rooted in medical analogies, the concept was both essential and acceptable at the time, especially the late 1930s. The Great Depression had made it clear to almost all that the problems facing the poorest Canadians were being compounded by inadequate housing and a severe shortage of community amenities.[31] The year 1935 saw Canada's first significant federal housing legislation, the Dominion Housing Act, which declared that "individuals and families would benefit both physically and emotionally from improved habitation." This was followed by the 1944 amendments to the National Housing Act.

In the 1960s, Toronto, like other North American cities, looked with alarm at the deteriorating housing in its downtown core and set about creating open spaces as a sleek expression of modernity. Yet the city made little note of the lower-income working-class people living in the areas it proposed to clear. As a consequence, history was either erased, or enshrined in museums or designated historic districts. Urban renewal too often meant disrupting memories and discounting the human factor.

Why was Kensington Market different? There are three principal reasons. First, the neighbourhood had been evolving organically, *without* planning, ever since its years as a Jewish enclave in the early twentieth century, and it had continued to serve as a mecca for immigrants, from Eastern Europeans to Italians to Portuguese to Jamaicans to South and Central Americans and then to Asians. Each immigrant group had brought with it a distinctive home culture and tried tenaciously to hold on to it. Kensington Market has always belonged to people whose priority has been survival, not architectural beauty. Second, the Market has a long history of activism. "Urban renewal in Toronto and elsewhere had sometimes been like a red rag to a bulldozer – an invitation to wholesale clearance. That was exactly what the people of Kensington didn't want."[32] Third, unlike in other neighbourhoods, the people of Kensington Market wanted urban renewal to solve problems (such as traffic congestion and poor sanitation) *without* damaging the community's spirit.

Despite the general understanding that the unique ambiance of an open-air market was worth preserving, the professionals (planners and city officials; planning boards, urban renewal authority, housing authority, and conservation authority) and local residents (homeowners, tenants, and business owners) split on two elementary issues: First, what was urban renewal? Second, what was the special character of Kensington Market?

In Kensington Market, the goals of urban renewal were never fully explained to those most directly affected. Discussions about the social impact of sophisticated renewal schemes were invariably laced with planning jargon. For planners, urban renewal generally meant redevelopment in order to solve physical, health, and social problems. For some residents of the Market, especially property owners and tenants, it meant the renovation or demolition of housing – or, put more simply, a threat to their way of life.

Another taken-for-granted issue is neighbourhood character, or special identity. Both terms are rather loaded. Politicians and planners tend to favour pedestrian malls, expanded institutional use, more parking space, or, worse, total clearance. So the solutions they proposed for Kensington Market came as no surprise. They called for a multistorey distribution centre to be built on the Market's periphery in order to reduce vehicular traffic. Merchandise would be stored there and moved to and from individual shops by handcart. Some of the market streets could then be developed as pedestrian malls, without having to open up any back lanes (which would have required the demolition of adjacent houses). Parking facilities would be provided as well. Finally, space would be provided to relocate noxious but valued market businesses such as fish processing.

But for the residents, the Market was their home, a place where they had invested their hearts and their labour. And key to their neighbourhood's identity was its visual character. Most of them wanted the Market to be preserved and improved, but in such a way that its visual characteristics were preserved or restored. According to the Kensington Area Residents Association (KARA), this meant "that the market's community service must be continued while ways to reduce the problems associated with the market are developed … [The community desires] to identify and protect the best visual characteristics of the area and to restore the parts of the area which have deteriorated and to ensure that new development enhances the visual appearance of the area."[33] The heart of this observation was that the residents had a real and personal connection with Kensington Market, where they were building personal and community history.

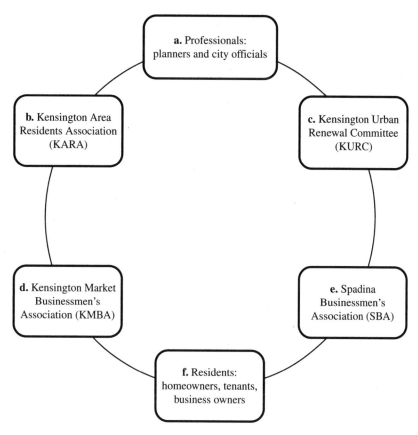

Figure 2.3. Different parties involved in urban renewal planning in Kensington.

The planners acknowledged the attractiveness of the Market, but mainly from a professional standpoint: "The market is a lively and interesting place ... The present trend of improvements to the commercial buildings of the market is indicative of the merchants' interest which will, no doubt, be further encouraged by the participation of public agencies in a renewal scheme." Furthermore, "some of the residential streets have a pleasant scale, particularly the group of buildings around Bellevue square; the domes and towers of the synagogues; the fire tower and the old St Stephen's Church are valuable visual assets which help to give the area an identity."[34] Thus, the vernacular structures, especially the ordinary residences with little architectural significance, matched planners' "pleasant scale."

Urban renewal planning in Kensington Market ended in 1970 when the federal government announced a financial freeze on further urban renewal projects, a year after the Board of Control confirmed the Planning Board's decision not to continue the Kensington Market project. The failure to implement what had been studied, discussed, and planned over almost a decade turned out to be good news for the Market's residents. Paradoxically, the first objective listed in the Urban Renewal Scheme – that the existing community be retained and strengthened – was actually met by *not* implementing the proposed plan.

Over the following decades, the sources of conflict – disparate views of urban renewal and redevelopment, debates over neighbourhood character and identity, culture and language issues, and so on – persisted as efforts were made to redevelop Kensington Market even while preserving it. Some of these efforts succeeded, others did not. Public participation was key to the success (or failure) of any planning initiatives. In the 1970s, planners proposed that the Market be declared a priority area for a federal funding initiative – the Neighbourhood Improvement Program (NIP) – to improve community facilities. But when it came to involving the local community, that proposal met opposition: the residents perceived it as "yet another 'renewal scheme.'"[35] The initiative was eventually approved and implemented, but only after long discussion. Then in the 1980s, planners again raised the Kensington Revitalization Plan.

Official versus Vernacular: Historic Designation of Kensington Market

A brief examination of Kensington Market's designation as a historic site seems relevant. In 2005, with the support of a neighbourhood committee chaired by Marcia Cuthbert, Dr Carlos Teixeira submitted

Kensington Market to the HSMBC for possible designation as a historic district.[36] Within the framework of HSMBC, Kensington Market was assessed first by relevant HSMBC Criteria/Guidelines, and second in terms of the neighbourhood's historic value. The following HSMBC criteria and guidelines applied to the Market:

- Criterion 1 (b), *illustrates or symbolizes in whole or in part a cultural tradition, a way of life, or ideas important in the development of Canada.*
- Specific Guideline 3.6 on Historic Districts, 1 (b) *a group of buildings, structure and open spaces, none of which may be of individual historical significance, but which together comprise an outstanding example of structures of technological or social significance,* and 1 (c) *a group of buildings, structures and open spaces which share uncommonly strong associations with individuals, events and themes of national significance.*
- Specific Guideline 5.4 on Ethnic and Religious Groups: *The Board will assess the national historic significance of places, persons and events associated with the experience of ethnic or religious groups in Canada, rather than advocating an approach that would consider the commemoration of ethnic or religious groups themselves.*

Regarding *Historic Values of the Place,* Kensington Market reflects important historical themes in Canada relating to urban migration and settlement patterns, the development of small businesses and entrepreneurs as a fundamental part of Canada's economic growth, the formation of cultural and religious identity through community organizations, and the expression of social and cultural history through a specific vernacular architecture characteristic of the neighbourhood (Figures 2.4 and 2.5).[37]

In the Canadian context, a historic district of national significance must, above all, have a "sense of history": there must be few intrusive elements, and the district's historic characteristics must predominate and set it apart from the area immediately surrounding it. According to the HSMBC, six aspects come into play: location, setting, design, material, use, and association.[38] As a reception area for waves of newcomers to Canada, Kensington Market has developed through constant flux. Its beginnings in the nineteenth century established the *location* and *setting* of the present neighbourhood. Changes in the economic situations and cultural influences of the arriving immigrants resulted in a commercial vernacular architecture with unique *design*

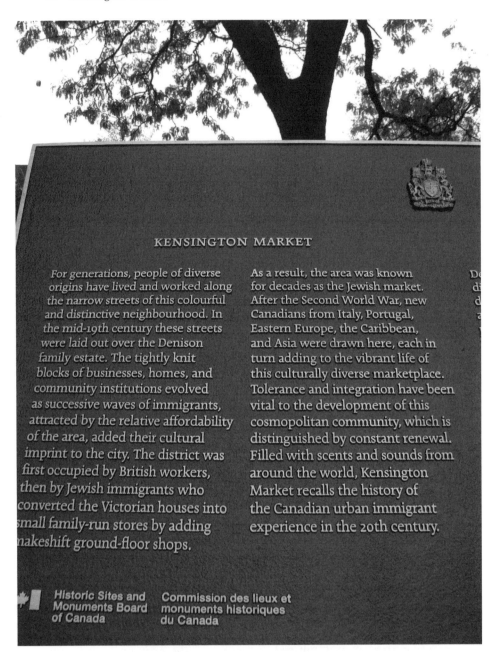

KENSINGTON MARKET

For generations, people of diverse origins have lived and worked along the narrow streets of this colourful and distinctive neighbourhood. In the mid-19th century these streets were laid out over the Denison family estate. The tightly knit blocks of businesses, homes, and community institutions evolved as successive waves of immigrants, attracted by the relative affordability of the area, added their cultural imprint to the city. The district was first occupied by British workers, then by Jewish immigrants who converted the Victorian houses into small family-run stores by adding makeshift ground-floor shops.

As a result, the area was known for decades as the Jewish market. After the Second World War, new Canadians from Italy, Portugal, Eastern Europe, the Caribbean, and Asia were drawn here, each in turn adding to the vibrant life of this culturally diverse marketplace. Tolerance and integration have been vital to the development of this cosmopolitan community, which is distinguished by constant renewal. Filled with scents and sounds from around the world, Kensington Market recalls the history of the Canadian urban immigrant experience in the 20th century.

Historic Sites and Monuments Board of Canada   Commission des lieux et monuments historiques du Canada

Figure 2.4. Kensington Market plaque, in Bellevue Park near the corner of Denison Square and Augusta Avenue.

Figure 2.5. Kensington Market plaque, in Bellevue Park near the corner of Denison Square and Augusta Avenue.

and *material* specific to Kensington Market. Each successive wave of immigration to Toronto over the twentieth century added layers of cultural richness and variety. Kensington Market's internal dynamism and living colour account for its distinctive character, especially with regard to its unplanned evolution as an autonomous market in the heart of Toronto. The area's vibrant atmosphere is directly *associated* with its ethnic diversity, which continues to change as new immigrants arrive.[39]

Different waves of immigrants brought architectural styles that were unique to their home cultures. Houses were turned into shops based in part on the owners' ethnic origins, aesthetic tastes, and cultural attachments. Yet the original buildings from the 1880s and 1890s still stand (Figure 2.6). The more recent additions to the old Victorian houses have

Figure 2.6. Original houses on Kensington Avenue.

given Kensington Market its distinctive *location*, defined by the HSMBC as the linkages among buildings, structures, sites, objects, and spaces that continue to stand where they were first raised. The resulting landscapes reflect Kensington's evolution from a Jewish market to today's multicultural commercial district. The proximity of the buildings to the narrow streets, especially along Baldwin (Figure 2.7) and parts of Augusta, points to how Kensington Market developed differently from other areas of Toronto.

The *setting*, the distinctive and readily definable boundaries and focal points, also remains. Kensington Market is easily distinguishable from the surrounding area because of its density, haphazardness, and development as a commercial area separate from

Figure 2.7. Baldwin streetscape.

Toronto's more familiar commercial streetscapes along major streets and avenues. At each of the street entrances into the Market, there is a clear change from larger, purpose-built commercial buildings to smaller, converted ones. The area's distinctive high density on small lots began to emerge in the late nineteenth century and continued throughout the Jewish influx into the area. Without the Jewish presence, the Market's residential buildings probably would not have been converted into small shops, bakeries, and grocery stores. The Portuguese and later immigrants to the neighbourhood carried on the Jewish tradition.

The third attribute, *design,* relates to a visual cohesiveness displayed through similar and dissimilar forms, plans, spaces, structures, and perhaps styles. Kensington Market evolved informally and organically beginning in the nineteenth century. The streets' two- and two-and-a-half-storey Victorian rowhouses have been modified to suit the needs of businesses. A new vernacular architecture has developed from the streets' familiar row houses. The countless additions, partial demolitions, and constructions since Jewish settlement in the early twentieth century have resulted in a concentration of buildings and spaces that together form a unique eclectic aesthetic. The permanent additions of brick were built mainly from the 1910s to the 1930s, when the Jewish Market was in its heyday (Figure 2.8).

Most of the shops in the Market have canopies and awnings stretching out over the narrow sidewalks. When the city threatened to remove them in the early 1980s, the neighbourhood fought to retain them as a defining feature. Baldwin Street and Augusta Avenue, more so than Kensington Avenue, still have many canopies to shelter the produce being sold in front of the shops. Another solution chosen by many shop owners has been to convert the temporary canopies into permanent albeit makeshift enclosed shelters for their shops. On Augusta Avenue, there are examples of these less permanent single-storey garage-like additions to the houses. They are unheated and are made of corrugated metal and pressboard. Some have remained structurally unchanged for thirty years.

If the structures added to the buildings are the vernacular architecture of the Jewish phase, the vibrant colours of the buildings can be attributed to the Portuguese. Many of the storefronts and signs have been painted in rich patterns and shapes.[40] Adding to the area's vibrancy is

Figure 2.8. 176 Baldwin Street is a classic example of vernacular architecture in Kensington Market. When European Quality Meat and Sausages arrived in the Market in 1964, it occupied 178 Baldwin Street. Later it was composed of two old row houses. The original site at 178 Baldwin was used as a cutting and preparation room. European Quality Meat and Sausages closed its Kensington store in 2012.

the graffiti found on almost every building (Figure 2.9). As a group of low-rise buildings in a melange of ad hoc designs formed over the past century, the district reflects a unique commercial vernacular architecture that does not conform to the urban architecture beyond the district. The design of each shop has changed with the store ownership to express a particular cultural tradition. Yet the overall scale and style of the modified late-nineteenth-century houses has been retained, despite these surface treatments, and even though some buildings have been replaced.

Figure 2.9. Grafitti on the north wall of 52 and 54 Kensington Avenue. According to Doug Taylor, this type of art was created with spray cans, using no brush work. Smaller details were accomplished by holding the can closer to the wall.

Related to design is *material,* defined as the sense of place conveyed through the use of similar or dissimilar materials or techniques. Kensington Market has a somewhat dilapidated appearance, with corrugated metal panels, pressboard, plywood, grates, metal grills, and even recycled window frames.

Many of the early additions to the Victorian row houses were built using similar brick, notably for the buildings along Kensington Avenue and Baldwin Street. In most cases the additions were later painted in bright colours and covered with large signs. More makeshift awnings and enclosures, as seen on Augusta Avenue, were built using a variety of building materials. The patchwork construction and the variety of materials for enclosing the shopfronts are evident along all of the area's streets. These patchwork add-ons appear only within the district and sharply distinguish it from the shops along Spadina Avenue.[41]

Toronto's Lower East Side

Historic significance entails more than materiality. Two other attributes – *use* and *associations* – point to a deeper, social layer. *Use* refers to a sense of cohesiveness based on activities common to many or all of the buildings. In Kensington Market, most of the buildings support the market function directly or indirectly. *Association* relates to the links between a district and the historic theme(s) or event(s) for which that district is significant. The principal historical themes associated with Kensington Market are immigration and the experience of ethno-cultural immigrant life in urban Canada. Kensington Market has been home to more than twenty different cultural communities. In the Market's early years, when it was largely Jewish, few Gentiles lived in the area. By the 1930s, a few Italians and Eastern Europeans had located there. The Sanci family, who moved into Kensington Market in 1937 (after establishing the family business in 1914 in the Ward), were the first Italians on Kensington Avenue to open a fruit store. After the Second World War, Eastern European, Portuguese, Afro-Caribbean, Chinese, and Vietnamese immigrants came to live in the Market. Each wave of immigrants has made its mark as it moved through the neighbourhood.

But remember that Kensington Market began as place of *survival.* Pushing a handcart or a food cart was a way to eke out a living. As Steven Speisman vividly points out, "peddling, tinkering and hawking were the best chance the immigrants had of breaking from the grinding poverty or routine and heavy work."[42] Few options were open for rising above menial labour, and many Jewish immigrants found themselves employed in the garment industry with the T. Eaton Company.

In the 1920s and 1930s, about 60,000 Jews lived around Kensington Market, worshipping at over thirty local synagogues.[43] Unless they were able to purchase their own homes, they faced substandard housing.[44] Because they didn't know how to seek redress for housing problems or were afraid to do so, they were easy marks for speculators. And because the value of the land was out of proportion to the rent, landlords cared little about maintaining their properties. Especially bad were the plumbing and drainage systems. Most houses had only a backyard privy, so windows could not be opened because of the stench. Especially dreadful were the overcrowded boarding houses. "In one case, 19 men slept in three rooms, and in another 7 men slept in a room seven by twelve."[45] Just as with the tenements in early-twentieth-century New York City, housing conditions linked Kensington Market early on with issues of social equity.[46] The question was whether to demolish or preserve housing that urban reformers – such as Jacob Riis, Lawrence Veiller, John Ihlder, Ernest Bohn, and Bleecker Marquette, in the context of late-nineteenth-century New York – described as "fetid, crowded," and as fostering disease (including tuberculosis), malnutrition, and crime as well as other social problems.[47]

Kensington – an Urban Neighbourhood, a Cultural Metaphor

Kensington Market's narrow streets and older housing stock have resulted in a neighbourhood of high density and mixed uses. The housing is largely attached homes and low-rise apartment buildings. The concept of "urban neighbourhood" merits a review here, given that planners' notions of it rarely coincide with those of the actual residents. Yi-Fu Tuan points out that "a district well defined by its physical characteristics and given a prominent name on the city plan may have no reality for the local people."[48] It is critically important to acknowledge this interpretive gap, for it raises a fundamental question for urban preservationists: What is worth preserving at a particular time and place?

According to Suzanne Keller, a neighbourhood is defined by its territory and its inhabitants.[49] The distinctiveness of a given neighbourhood arises from many things, including its geographical boundaries, the ethnic or cultural characteristics of the inhabitants, the psychological unity of people who feel they belong together, and the area's facilities for shopping, leisure, and learning. But the actual values of these things are difficult to assess independently. A key aspect of neighbourhoods that has yet to be adequately evaluated is people's sense of attachment, the special meaning they give to a place, their pride in living there; these can and do transcend a neighbourhood's physical amenities (or lack of them) and social desirability (or lack of it). "This attachment may be rooted in childhood experiences or family involvement with the area over a long period or in historical events endowing an area with a special meaning."[50]

Kensington Market is a cultural landscape, a *place*, where the built environment has been socially produced.[51] Regarding the social history of built forms, Anthony D. King writes that "buildings, indeed, the entire built environment, are essentially social and cultural products. Buildings result from social needs and accommodate a variety of functions – economic, social, political, religious and cultural. Their size, appearance, location and form are governed not simply by physical factors but by a society's ideas."[52] Carl Sauer and John Leighly's seminal interpretation of cultural landscapes reverberates to this day – such landscapes are "an amalgam of physical and cultural forms: culture is the agent and the natural area is the medium, the cultural landscape the result."[53]

When we trace the social history of Kensington Market, we find that it has always had its own interior life. Its people come from countries and regions where the street is a large part of daily life. Also, new Canadians have a natural tendency to form tightly knit communities centred on their home countries, from which people have brought a wealth of worldly experiences, and they tenaciously hold on to their faith, language, diet, culture, and customs. In these communities flourishes a spirit of *survivance*, "an idea of cultural maintenance corresponding to the desire to preserve religion, language and customs."[54] As Nadekeube Giguere observes: "They were not searching for a new way of life but for a better means of carrying out the old way of life."[55]

The influx of Jewish immigrants a century ago generated a strong demand for shops that sold Eastern European merchandise and that provided service in the native language of the immigrants. In the Market, people could start a business with relatively little capital. There was little oversight over the design of the district; thus, the first floors of many houses were converted into shops, with the upper floors retained as residences.

Figure 2.10. Corner of Baldwin Street and Augusta Avenue. The owner of Casa Acoreana came from the Azores. Although somewhat dilapidated, this small café is a sweet place to reminisce. Many old people sit here every day watching the bustling Kensington Market and drinking good coffee.

Jewish Europeans continued to be the dominant residential group until the 1950s and would remain the dominant business group into the 1960s. That said, by 1941 – and certainly by 1950, when the Jewish community began to migrate to the north and west – the area had become a Babel of diverse immigrant communities, including Portuguese, Ukrainians, Hungarians, and Italians. By the 1960s, Portuguese from the Azores were the area's dominant ethnic group (Figure 2.10); they were followed in the 1970s and 1980s by an influx of Asian immigrants (Figure 2.11).[56] The immigrant cultures encountered the cultures

Figure 2.11. Corner of Spadina Avenue and Baldwin Street. In the early 1990s, when Jewish merchants moved into the area from the Ward, Kensington was known as the Jewish Market. Even today, after waves of immigration, the Chinese refer to it as the Jewish Market. So says this sign, with "Chinatown" below.

that had already taken root there. The resulting interactions sometimes generated cultural tensions; more often, though, they brought out multiple senses of place that reflected the pulsating energy of Kensington Market and that shaped the people who had made it their home.

Chapter Three

Collective Memory and Kensington Market

What makes it so unique is that every day somebody will come in, and share stories with us, of their memories, of having their first meal in Canada at United Bakers on Spadina, knowing my father, knowing my grandfather and grandmother. Even today, a lot of the older population are passing away, but there are still, not many, but a handful of them that remember ... particularly the older population, people that know my grandfather, who ... grew up on Spadina Avenue, who are now in their seventies. Even Mel Lastman, who grew up in Kensington Market, came here regularly. Sure, Mel comes here all the time ... You know, they grew up in Kensington, and they grew up with United Bakers as part of their life. And they continue to eat here, and they continue to share stories, and it is a really wonderful feeling to have so many people come here to feel the connection to our family, to feel the connection to our lives.

– Ruthie Ladovsky, United Bakers
Dairy Restaurant

Fifty years ago when we started our business, the owners knew all their customers. I think that every single customer should be recognized. If you have customers supporting you over the years, they deserve some kind of recognition. The only way we can recognize their shopping habits, their shopping pattern, if they come to my store, is to try to give them a discount, and make them feel important, and that is what I don't see in today's world, that the customer is not made important. Profit is important to stay in business, but it is not *always* important. Fifty years or forty years ago, when you came down to Kensington Market, the owner worked every day. He knew what the customers wanted, and he carried the products the customers needed. And he had that personal love and that attachment to his customers.

– Tom Mihalik, Tom's Place

Kensington Market started as a Jewish neighbourhood partly because the housing was affordable but also because the T. Eaton Company provided job opportunities. Until the 1960s, Jews were the dominant ethnic group, and they did much to shape the Market's development. Between 1901 and 1931, the population of Toronto quadrupled, from 156,000 to 631,000. The Jewish population expanded by almost twelve in those same years, from 3,000 to 35,000. By 1931, Jews were Toronto's largest non-British group, accounting for 7.2 per cent of the population. The 1951 census found that Jews were still the city's largest ethnic group, at 6 per cent.

At the time, Spadina Avenue was the "counterculture" to the more sober Upper Canadian mainstream – economically, politically, culturally, ethnically, linguistically.[1] These forces coalescing along Spadina were greatly strengthened by the Jewish community, whose members continued to observe their religion, building new synagogues and expanding old ones. Secular cultural organizations flourished alongside religious ones: Yiddish theatre, Yiddish literature. All of this contributed socially, commercially, religiously, intellectually, and culturally to the evolution of Kensington Market; it also profoundly shaped Toronto's character.

Memory and Place: Authentic Place-Making in Kensington Market

Aristotle wrote in *De Memoria et Reminiscentia:* "Place is [the] innermost motionless boundary of what contains. It is thought to be a kind of surface, and as it were a vessel, i.e., a container of things. Place is coincident with the thing, for boundaries are coincident with the bounded (*perichon*, i.e. having or holding around)."[2] So "the power of place is a remarkable one, as the hold is held." Memory is of the past: someone who is actively engaged in remembering always says in his soul that he heard, perceived, or thought this before. This, according to Aristotle, indicates a state of affection.[3]

Long after, in *De Oratore,* Cicero introduced the mnemonic of *loci* (places), as well as the notion of memory as inner writing: "The first step was to imprint on the memory a series of loci or places." A *locus* is a place easily grasped by the memory, such as a house, an intercolumnar space, a corner, an arch, or the like.[4] The formation of *loci* is of the greatest importance, for those same *loci* can be used again and again to remember different material. Almost a century after Cicero, in *Institutio Oratoria,* Quintilian suggested why places help memory: experience tells us that places call up associations in memory.

Frances A. Yates in *The Art of Memory* traces the artistic feeling for place, beginning with the classical tradition: "Peter of Ravenna gives it [place rules] much earlier. A memory *locus,* which is to contain a memory image, must not be larger than a man can reach; this is illustrated by a cut of a human image on a locus, reaching upwards and sideways to demonstrate the right proportions of the locus in relation to the image. This rule grows out of the artistic feeling for space, lighting, distance, in memory in the classical place rules."[5]

Edward Casey suggests a radically inclusive notion of space that would allow us to account for the entire landscape of a given place.[6] "The affinity between memory and place calls for each other."[7] He writes that places furnish convenient points of attachment for memories; furthermore, they provide locations in which remembered actions can deploy themselves – or more precisely, places are solidified locations for remembered contents, and as such they situate what we remember.[8]

In this regard, place and memory are mutually selected: a given place will stimulate certain memories while discouraging others; at the same time, memories seek out particular places as their natural habitats. How, then, is interaction between memory and place part of place-making and ultimately of *senses of place*? Kensington Market evolved organically, which is to say that the place-making there occurred without deliberation. "If place-making is a way of constructing the past, a venerable means of doing human history, it is also a way of constructing social traditions and, in the process, personal and social identities."[9] This is an active endeavour; from this it follows that place-making, fundamentally, means the building of multiple relationships. Emotions play an important role in relationship-building, for "life is inherently spatial, and inherently emotional."[10] Kay Anderson and Susan Smith's editorial "Emotional Geographies" (2001) opened up new territory not only in geography but also in fields that deal with spatial elements of our environment, such as planning.[11] On that territory, emotional attachment to a place becomes critical. More recently, James Opp and John Walsh in *Placing Memory and Remembering Place in Canada* have focused more directly on the "palpable immediacy of local places."[12]

In Kensington Market, the tangible and intangible qualities that give place special meaning are strong. There, people's emphasis is on common responses to common needs rather than on abstract notions of authenticity. More importantly, the Market has evolved in such a way that its "integrity," its *genius loci,* has been kept alive.[13] The Market has generated its own distinctive staying power, a power rooted in personal and community memories.

In my search for the "spirit" of Kensington Market, I have explored every corner of it, including the back alleys. I have taken building-by-building and street-by-street photographs, comparing them with historic photographs and cross-referencing them with city records; I have talked with store owners and visitors; I have participated in the Sabbath service at the Kiev synagogue on Saturdays and celebrated Kiddush with the congregants afterwards; and so on. Through close observation at different times of day, I have found that every detail comes alive with rich texture, that every encounter brings out fascinating stories, that every building records family and community memories – social memory in the religious place, multiple layers of memory in the same locale, memories moving with place, memories lingering even after place is gone. The traces that remain of these sites of memory bring alive what is invisible.

The Landscape of Spirit: Kiev Synagogue, 25 Bellevue Avenue

The need to preserve their Jewish identity was strong, and, even during their most arduous times, the need for spiritual outlets and ritual was uppermost in their minds.

– Goldie Liebman, "Three
Toronto Synagogues"[14]

The world of space surrounds our existence. It is but a part of living, the rest is time. Things are the shore, the voyage is in time … When we learn to understand that it is the spatial things that are constantly running out, we realize that time is that which never expires, that it is the world of space which is rolling through the infinite expanse of time.

– Abraham Joshua Heschel,
The Sabbath[15]

A Humble Beginning

The synagogues of Kensington Market were an outgrowth of working-class Jewish community-building.[16] They reflected an innate need to uphold Jewish identity. The congregation of Rodfei Sholem Anshei Kiev (Pursuer of Peace, Men of Kiev), commonly known as the Kiever, dates back to 1912. Some of the founders, living in the Ward at the time, were recent working-class immigrants – carpenters, blacksmiths, tailors, peddlers – and they had few resources to build a place of worship. They rented a house on Centre Avenue in the Ward. Then in 1917, they acquired a house at 25 Bellevue Avenue in Kensington Market. The congregation had enough confidence in Jewish expertise to employ an architect of their own faith to design the building.[17] The structure would be completed in 1927.

In Kensington Market, a pattern had been established: Jews from specific regions (*Landsmanschaften*) or self-help organizations would band together to worship, forming synagogues with names like Anshe Kielce (Men of Kielc), Romanisha Shule, Anshei England (Hebrew Men of England), and Anshe Minsk. Writes David Pinkus: "Although the first waves of Eastern European Jews were concerned with creating a proper religious environment, they were not inclined to align themselves with the larger synagogues. Instead, upon arrival they initiated smaller Shuls, called Shetels. From each ethnic sector a group of males from the same village, town or city would organize their own house of worship to maintain their unique customs."[18] The founding of the Kiev reflected this pattern in the working-class Kensington Market of the early twentieth century. It "served as safety valves and security blankets for the immigrants as well as integrating the social and religious life of the neighborhood. They were definitely meeting places where landsmen could find understanding and moral support from their fellow congregants."[19]

Judaism emphasizes an ultimate commitment to God – "the yearn[ing] for spiritual living, the awareness of ubiquitous mystery, the noble nostalgia for God, all are indispensable parts of Jewish soul"[20] – as well as an ultimate reciprocity, a partnership of God and humans. "God is not detached from or indifferent to our joys and griefs. Authentic vital needs of man's body and soul are a divine concern. That is why human life is holy. God is a partner and a partisan in man's struggle for justice, peace, and holiness and it is because of his being in need of man that He entered a covenant with him for all time, a mutual bond embracing God and man, a relationship to which God, not only man, is committed."[21] To build a structure to support and practise such faith requires an equal amount of commitment. "Raising an edifice was an act of worship in which the feelings and senses of a people were deeply engaged."[22]

There is no clear evidence that when Benjamin Swartz, a novice Jewish architect, designed the Kiev, his faith aligned with his design (Figures 3.1, 3.2, 3.3, and 3.4). We do know that the Kiever brought

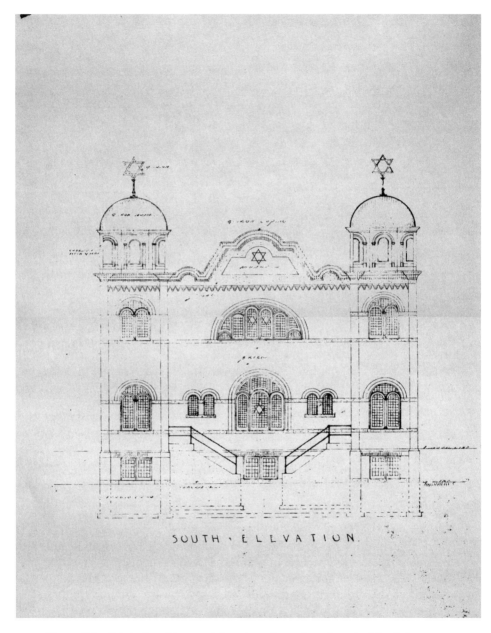

Figure 3.1. Original architectural drawing of exterior of south side of the Kiev. This was done by Benjamin Swartz, c. 1923. Swartz combined arches, ironwork, red brick, and decorative stained-glass windows. Source: Ontario Jewish Archives, Accession #2004-1/6.

Figure 3.2. Exterior of south side of the Kiev.

with them a strong sense of community from their home culture. The surviving material culture attests to this.

Eternity into Temporality: Spirit of Space[23]

As the illustrations show, the Kiev is in classic Middle Eastern style and combines Byzantine, Romanesque, and Art Deco elements. It is a modest example of the style for synagogues established in Toronto at the time. By the mid-1930s, Toronto synagogues were following a certain formula – twin-towered, with round-headed openings and an interior dome.[24] The

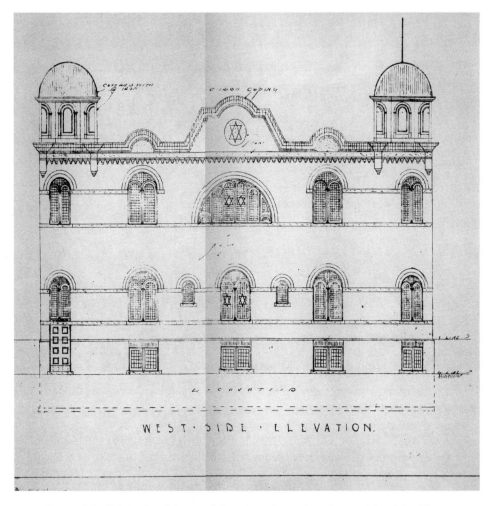

Figure 3.3. Original architectural drawing of exterior of west side of the Kiev. The entrances to the synagogue are to the sides of the stair towers, resulting in a less majestic or imposing entrance. Source: Ontario Jewish Archives, Accession #2004-1/6.

Figure 3.4 West side of the Kiev.

interior, like that of all synagogues built in Toronto since Holy Blossom on Bond Street,[25] has a central dome over the sanctuary. Also like its other traditional contemporaries, it has a hand-carved ark at the eastern end and the *bimah* in the centre. (Figure 3.5) "This is what the Sovereign Lord says, Although I sent them far away among the nations and scattered them among the countries, yet for a little while I have been a sanctuary for them in the countries where they have gone."[26] Some distinct architectural features, however, were incorporated into the Kiev, including twin Byzantine-style domes, pastel and white trim, a decorative extended parapet, and four different styles of arched windows. Also, the entrances are located in the stair towers, with lower elevation to remind people of its humble origin.

The *bimah*, being the focus of attention during worship, exercised a decisive influence on the Kiev's design, including its lighting. The hall is a simple rectangle; the roof is low in slope and simple in profile, with no towers.[27] The *bimah* itself stands along the main axis and is emphasized by distinctive architectural features such as a skylight, a lantern, and pillars. The *bimah* table, built of wood,[28] is raised on a platform with an enclosing railing (Figure 3.6). The officiant reads the Torah scrolls from there and leads the congregation in turning towards Jerusalem during prayers. The platform follows a post-Talmudic tradition by allowing the prayers to be carried "out

Figure 3.5. Interior of the Kiev.

Figure 3.6. View from the *bimah* facing east. Services and Torah readings are led from this platform. Source: Ontario Jewish Archives, #311.

of the depth."[29] A central *bimah* also allows for interaction between the building and the worshippers.

At the eastern end of the bare wall, the Ark stands alone. Here the Torah scrolls, bounded in strips of fabric, are encased in a cloth cover adorned with a silver Torah shield. The Ark is covered by a curtain, which is likened to the veil that divided the Holy of Holies at the Temple. The Eternal Light, a symbol of the Law that Jews must keep alive, hangs in front of the Ark: it was first lit at the synagogue's dedication when the Torah scrolls were placed in the Ark. Orthodox Jews usually do not use electricity on the Sabbath, so the dome, the *huppa* frame, functions as an acoustic device for the individual reading.

The windows in the walls are small, to allow for the later addition of side annexes high enough to hold standing adults without blocking the main prayer hall windows. The small windows result in an almost sober mood. Besides the natural light, there are artificial lights. The candelabra near the *bimah* railing adds light to the centre of the prayer hall.

"Pious Jews at prayer may be indifferent to beauty in the synagogue, but they are sensitive to the correct arrangement of synagogue furnishings. The ritual furniture is connected to liturgy and to ancestral traditions that help maintain the cohesion of the minority group."[30] The Kiev's material culture clarifies social roles and relations.[31] While mainly a religious place, it also presents a Jewish interpretation of social relations. The Women's Auxiliary, for example, is separated from the men's congregation (Figure 3.7).

Figure 3.7. Women's Auxiliary. The space is lit by the coloured semicircular window in the central bay of the western facade. The mullions divide the large opening, recalling the narrow arches of the tower windows. From here, we see murals painted by the Silverstein family, stained-glass windows, and the men's seating area in the sanctuary. The seats with the best view of the *bimah* are numbered in multiples of eighteen, the number symbolizing life.

Throughout the synagogue are memorial plaques for those who have contributed to the Kiev. Family members donate money in the name of their deceased relatives to pay for the synagogue's various ornaments. See, for example, Figures 3.8 and 3.9.

In the early 1970s, the Kiev began to deteriorate: as a result of water damage and a termite infestation, the structure was in desperate need of repair. Because of severely ailing finances, it ran the risk of being sold. But the determination to preserve the Kiev was strong: "The community should have the building not only for its inherent historical value, but also because it would provide a physical environment where youth could identify their roots, to see their parent's milieu and what motivated previous generations."[32] A Restoration Committee, led by

Figure 3.8. Name of Mr and Mrs Harry Litvak. Their names are carved into the stone on the exterior of the southern side of the Kiev.

Figure 3.9. Mr and Mrs Harry Litvak, 6 May 1939. Source: Ontario Jewish Archives, photo #531.

Sol Edell and Albert Latner, was formed, and that committee[33] was able to raise enough money for the restoration, which began in 1981. This involved replacing doors and windows to match the originals. Also, the social hall was renovated and the exterior trim and interior walls were repainted. The restoration was completed by the mid-1980s.[34]

In 1979, the Ontario government designated the Kiev as a historical site under the Ontario Heritage Act – the first building of Jewish significance to be given this designation in Ontario. It is historically unique because of its distinctive architectural features and because it was the first synagogue built by Ukrainian Jews who had escaped from Czarist Russia. The Kiev's current rabbi, Aaron Levy, is excited about building traditional and progressive Jewish life in Toronto through Makom,[35] a grassroots, downtown Jewish community: "We are creating an inclusive and diverse space committed to Jewish learning, arts and culture, spirited prayer and ritual, and social and environmental activism."[36] Jane Jacobs's adage "new ideas need old buildings" resonates in his words.

The Kiev holds the collective memories of families and community. Its mainly religious functions long ago expanded into the social and cultural arenas of a Jewish community that has changed demographically over the past fifty years. Now, what about sites that have vanished or have been physically transformed? Can they still hold memories?

The Intellectual Landscape – Hyman's Bookstore, 412 Spadina Avenue

The only people my parents would not allow in the store were the communists. Everyone else, and their political viewpoints from the right to the left, including the religious, was welcome there. They discussed Israeli politics and Canadian, too, but mostly whatever affected the Jewish community. It was a place where people of varying opinions could come and exchange ideas.

– Gurion Yman, son of Ben Zion Hyman[37]

Essential to any Jewish community is a place to study, and synagogues typically provide it. But there was another venue that left an indelible mark on the intellectual landscape of Jewish Kensington – Hyman's Book & Art Shop, commonly known as Hyman's Bookstore, at 412 Spadina Avenue (Figure 3.10). There, a Jewish intellectual and his

Figure 3.10. Ben Zion Hyman in front of Hyman's Book & Art Shop at 371 Spadina Avenue in the 1930s. Source: Ontario Jewish Archives # 1171.

business-savvy wife fostered the intellectual life of Jewish immigrants in the early twentieth century.

Ben Zion Hyman was born around 1891 in what is now Belarus. His family was too poor to buy books, but he often visited his town's small Jewish library. He loved poetry, and he satisfied his yearning to own a book of Chayim Nachman Bialik's poems by copying an entire volume of them into a school notebook.[38] He studied electrical engineering at Odessa Polytechnic University, graduating in 1912. Having a gift for languages,[39] on his voyage to the New World, he studied English "with an English newspaper and a Russian–English, English–Russian dictionary." In Canada, he graduated from the University of Toronto in 1918 with a degree in electrical engineering. There was little prospect of securing a job that suited his talents, so he and Fanny (*née* Konstantynowsky) opened a bookstore at 371 Spadina Avenue); soon after, they moved the store to 412 Spadina (Figures 3.11 and 3.12).

At the time, Spadina Avenue was at its zenith, and their shop was only a few steps from the Labor Lyceum, the headquarters for many dressmakers' and furriers' unions. Hyman's bookstore quickly drew people from every political persuasion, who would discuss politics for hours. Here one could feel the pulsating energy of a budding community, a hive of lofty ideas as well as ordinary concerns.

An avid bibliophile, Ben Zion sold books on a wide range of topics. His store was the first to carry a complete line of books in English, especially books on Jewish topics. For newly arrived immigrants who spoke little English, he offered books that would help them adapt intellectually and socially to their new environment. Parents brought

Figure 3.11. Ben Zion Hyman in his bookstore in 1924. Photo courtesy Gurion and Ruth Hyman.

Figure 3.12. Gurion Hyman outside Hyman's Bookstore in 1948. Photo courtesy Gurion Hyman.

in their children so that they could learn Jewish subjects in English. The bookstore supplied the Jewish schools with their texts. It was also a lending library – five cents per day at the time. Ben Zion was deeply committed to his community; once, when the local Jewish library did not have enough money to buy new books, he "stole" them from his own shop and placed them there.[40]

His store also sold tickets for a nearby Jewish theatre. And it sold products for accountants, such as ledger sheets and index cards. "Many accountants, especially those that had clients in the garment district on lower Spadina, liked dealing with Ben Zion."[41] Gurion Hyman remembers driving in his jalopy to deliver accounting supplies to the furriers and dressmakers, and also to the Labor Lyceum. The bookstore also sold a variety of Jewish ritual items: taleisim, tefillin, siddurim, mahzorim, candlesticks, menorahs. Ben Zion put his poetic talents to good use. He designed Jewish greeting cards, "many of which [he] made himself, pop-ups, with glistening 'diamond' dust (made from glass), with poetic greetings written anonymously by some of the poets and well-known writers of Jewish Toronto. He sold his greeting cards wholesale to many small cigar and convenience stores who had Jewish customers."[42]

Hyman's Bookstore remained on Spadina until 1972, two years after Fanny passed away. Those who shopped there have fond memories of the place, which continues to exist as the Jewish Public Library, 4600 Bathurst Street.

The Culinary Landscape: United Bakers Dairy Restaurant, 338 Spadina Avenue

The garment industry was a very vibrant industry... Everything was manufactured on Spadina Avenue. The needle trade was a very very important business on Spadina, and there were a lot of Jewish merchants who owned factories, manufactured their garments there, sold to all of the stores. So yes, United Bakers was a hub, because it was a centre not just for the garment industry, but really, the Bay Street lawyers would come over and have lunch at United, the physicians at Mount Sinai Hospital would come over and have lunch at United. The Toronto Jewish Congress at the time was over on Beverley Street, and they used to walk along D'Arcy Street, across Spadina Avenue, and they had lunch at United. The fur traders union was all in the area, and the Labor Lyceum was just north of us. So everybody that worked in the area would come and have lunch at United. It was a real meeting spot. The same as it is today.

– Ruthie Ladovsky, current owner of
United Bakers Dairy Restaurant

United Bakers Dairy Restaurant, Toronto's oldest Jewish restaurant, is laden with Jewish memories. Originally located at 338 Spadina Avenue, it has since moved to 506 Lawrence Avenue West, far from Kensington Market.

Aaron and Sarah Ladovsky, from Kielce, Poland, opened United Bakers Dairy Restaurant in 1912, at the corner of Terauley and Agnes Streets (near today's Bay and Dundas Streets) (Figure 3.13). Also in

Figure 3.13.   Rosie Green, Rosie Lieberman, Aaron Ladovsky, and Sarah Ladovsky, at United Bakers in 1921. Photo courtesy Ruthie Ladovsky.

1912, they founded the Toronto chapter of the Bakers and Confectionary Workers International Union of America. Then in 1913 they founded the Kieltzer Society of Toronto, an immigrant aid association. They brought the same activist and pioneering spirit to their business venture. Its location, 338 Spadina Avenue, was only a few steps from the Labor Lyceum, which at the time was the hub of the Jewish community. United Bakers became a political and social centre for heated debates and trade meetings. "A peek into the nearly one hundred year past [of United Bakers] tells us much about Jewish immigration to Canada and dietary practices among Jews."[43] Many United Bakers customers still remember their first meal in Canada – the restaurant has always provided a clean, warm, and comfortable environment for new immigrants.

United Bakers has a *chechshure* (i.e., it is under a rabbi's supervision) but is not officially kosher. It maintains its own *ruach*, a Hebrew word meaning both "wind" and "spirit." Being strictly dairy, it serves no meat. Thus, it caters to observant Jews and to non-kosher customers as well. Historically, Kielce had been the "bagel basket" of Europe. "Aaron and his brother Lazar had trained as bakers in Poland, but most of the food served was, and continues to be, based on Sarah's original recipes."[44] The dairy soup, for example, follows a recipe from Kielce, which calls for sugar. So does the sweet and sour cabbage borscht, made on Fridays. For pickled herring, baked carp, and gefilte fish, United Bakers follows the Polish recipe by adding sugar, but also the Russian recipe by seasoning with salt and pepper. In this way, it accommodates customers from diverse backgrounds.[45]

> But here's an eatery still tied to its roots – United Bakers Dairy Restaurant – run with warmth and taste by the Ladovskys. Through the window I can see Herman, the aging elf, son of the original United Bakers. The last time I had a plate of his vegetarian chopped liver, he waved a copy of my letter to the editor of the *Canadian Jewish News* at me. "So you're still giving it to them!" he said, patting me on the back. His son Philip is beside him. Phil used to take kids on canoe trips in Temagami during the summers. He plays jazz piano when he's not behind the cash.[46]

In the 1980s, United Bakers left Spadina Avenue for Lawrence Avenue West, but miraculously, it has kept its integrity, and it continues to serve almost the same clientele – mainly Jewish, but from all walks of life. According to Ruthie:

> The continuity is in the tradition of not only serving traditional dairy dishes that newcomers to Canada might have enjoyed in the early 1900s, but building upon those dishes and offering newer menu items for the next generation. Our challenge is to consistently prepare the foods that our customers have always loved and associate with the United Bakers, and also to keep up with the demand for something new, at least once every ten years![47]

Yosef Hayim Yerushalmi's observation seems quite accurate with regard to this continuity at United Bakers: "Here in the course of a meal around the family table, ritual, liturgy, and even culinary elements are orchestrated to transmit a vital past from one generation to the next."[48] At United Bakers, the connection between people and their place endures.

Figure 3.14.   Ruthie, Herman, and Philip Ladovsky in 1999. The second and third generations of United Bakers. Photo courtesy Ruthie Ladovsky.

The Market[49]

I walked down to Kensington Market,
Bought me a fish to fry;
I went to the Silver Dollar,
Looked a stranger in the eye

– Murray McLauchlan, "Down by the
Henry Moore" (1975)[50]

The influx of Jewish immigrants created a strong demand for stores that sold Eastern Europe merchandise and offered services in the native tongue of the shoppers. The Market provided an opportunity to start a business with relatively little capital investment. There was little control over the design of the non-residential district, so the first floors of many houses were converted to shops, and the upper floors retained as residences. When the Jewish community slowly migrated to the north and west in the 1950s, the Market became a Babel of diverse immigrant communities, including Portuguese, Ukrainians, Hungarians, and Italians. The immigrant cultures and Canadian culture interacted. These interactions sometimes created tensions across cultural boundaries, but most often, they brought out multiple senses of place that reflected the pulsating energy of the Market, and ultimately a comprehensive package of its interior lives. Here are a few stores that have been in the Market for a few decades.

Sanci's, at 66 Kensington Avenue, is one of the oldest stores in Kensington Market. It was the first store in Toronto to import bananas and the first Italian merchant in predominantly Jewish Kensington Market. Salvatori (Sam) and Antonina Sanci bought the place in 1931, when it was surrounded by poultry dealers and kosher dairies. Before then, Sam had operated a fruit market at Queen and Bay. In 1937, now in Kensington, he extended the storefront, discreetly placing the outline of a cross on the brickwork as a sign of his religious identity (Figure 3.15). Most of the structure's interior is untouched to this day (Figure 3.16). David Borg, the

Figure 3.15. Sanci's: Brickwork of Greek Cross.

Figure 3.16. Interior of Sanci's Warehouse.

fourth generation of the Sanci family, walked me through, pinpoint-
ing various details while sharing his fond memories of Kensington
Market:

> It was my great-grandfather who started the business. He just sold
> bananas. He used to just bring his trucks down to the market, and sold
> them from his truck, and the cops did not let him do that. So he looked
> for a place, and he bought this property in 1922, or 1923. When the retail
> was booming in the 1940s, we sort of had the corner of the street [Kens-
> ington Avenue and Baldwin Street] ... I definitely feel part of a bigger
> community.

He describes the changes in the community in his lifetime:

> Well, Augusta and Kensington are pretty much two different communi-
> ties. It is not really one big community; it's kind of split up into smaller
> sections. I remember when I was walking along ... Kensington with my
> grandmother, we always got good deals on everything around. That was
> a lot of fun![51]

Tom's Place, a discount clothing store at 190 Baldwin Street, has
recently entered its fiftieth year (Figure 3.17). The store occupies
four old houses, with large skylights added to the roofs. Tom's Place
does not set firm prices and is known for its "semi-haggling." That
is a family tradition started half a century ago, when the store was
called William's Bargain Second Hand Store. Tom Mihalik, son of the
original owner, knows his customers and the Market so well that he
draws personal connections the moment you walk in the store. He
has always taken great pride in his family business and his customers and has never changed the store's facade. He reminisced about
his childhood and significant moments in his business venture:

> Kensington Market was called the Jewish Market by small entrepreneurs.
> A lot of those stores were homes, with people living upstairs and doing
> business downstairs. In 1968 when I came to work for my father, lot of
> stores were doing all their business outside, food stores, clothing stores,
> even the chicken stores. Now there are very few stores which are doing
> business outside, and most of the stores have become bigger. There are
> not many living upstairs. The beauty of Kensington was the rents were

Figure 3.17. Facade of Tom's Place.

low, so you could make a living. Plus you could live upstairs or downstairs. So you could do your business at home. A lot of people who were doing business were very hard-working.[52]

Perola Supermarket, 247 Augusta Avenue, is now almost half a century old and has become a well-known meeting spot for Toronto's Latin communities (Figures 3.18 and 3.19). Sidonio Freitas remembered how his parents started the store and what the Market was like:

The history of this store goes back to 1967. My father brought in this business. My mother came from Venezuela. The reason they came here

Figure 3.18. Perola Supermarket.

was because of the similarity in the language, the Portuguese and the Spanish – at least they can understand each other, as opposed to some places where they would not be able to because they spoke no English at all … We were the only place that had Latin products. Back in the late sixties and early seventies we had at one time eleven people working full time in the store, and it was a pretty crazy place back in those days.

I was five years old at the time, but I remember it was mainly Jews and Portuguese. There was really no anybody else at that time. Most of the businesses were Portuguese and Jewish.[interrupted][There was] so much character about the Market. It is the only open-air market of this type.

Figure 3.19. Interior of Perola Supermarket.

Over the years, fresh blood has been pumped into the market, younger people, or people with new ideas, such as Pedestrian Sundays ... A lot is going on here.[53]

Across the street at 190 Augusta Avenue is *House of Spice,* started in 1971. A family-owned business, it sells premium herbs and spices from around the world, as well as an assortment of hot sauces, sea salts, teas, coffees, spice blends, and other hard-to-locate specialty ingredients (Figure 3.20). Over the years, the owners have extended the building to the edge of the sidewalk, but the glass storefront remains

Figure 3.20. Interior of House of Spice.

(Figure 3.21). Carlos Pereira, the current owner, who immigrated from Portugal and has been in the area for thirty-five years, reminisces about the Market:

> A lot of friends, and a lot of hardships. The Market has changed a lot. Well, see, Kensington Market back in those days, you'd see ducks and chickens running around. The government has cleaned it up, which is a good thing, environment and health wise. You have to do that, right? I think it is for the good.[Sounds a bit reluctant] Everything is so expensive now, but Kensington Market is still one of the best places to come to shop ... It was a lot busier, people running everywhere, packed with people.[54]

Figure 3.21. Original Glass Front.

Another grocery store, Caribbean Corner, at 171 Baldwin Street, serves a mainly Jamaican clientele. The building was owned by David Kwasniewski in 1923 and then occupied by various families until 1957 (Figure 3.22 and 3.23). Baldwin Kosher Meat Market opened there in 1958 and remained in business until the 1970s. Yvonne Grant, the current owner, described the changes over the years:

When I first started in 1977, the store was on Kensington Avenue. Kensington Market was much different, much different. It had more ... [interruption]It used to have live chickens, more smelly, and the buildings were relatively more dilapidated. It has changed ... When I first came here, it was mostly Jewish, and then gradually, Portuguese came in, then Jamaicans. I

Figure 3.22. Caribbean Corner, seen from across Baldwin Street.

did a feasibility study and found this location. I wanted to make it a little corner of the Caribbean, which reminded me of home.[55]

Most of the stores have long-time customers. People come not just to shop, or to eat, but to see one another. The singular beauty of the Market lies in the profound sense that time is meeting humanity in a *place,* one where individual memories, desires, and hopes can be shared:

Oh, yeah, sometimes four generations come into the store. They share stories with me sometimes. Some people made friends here, because they come the same day each week, right here. I like that ... Some people who did not see each other for a long time, years and years. They come here, and they see each other. They get all excited!

Figure 3.23. Interior of Caribbean Corner.

Regarding how she runs the business:

> Basically … you react like a human being. It is not only money, money, money … Again, it just happened.[56]
>
> We have many old customers. We have customers who go back thirty-five or forty years … I get customers that I knew when they were kids, which is pretty wild … because they spend their lifetime here. I enjoy this whole business, luckily. I am not sure if my kids are interested in carrying on.

In a similar vein, Sidonio Freitas of Perola observes:

> This place has become a bit of a tradition for a lot of people …The Mexican consul is a customer here. It is nice to see a bunch of people come in and they meet here, saying "Hey, I have not seen you for a while." They meet and shop here, and they make friends, then they become known for many years. [Just as he is talking, a customer enters and says hello in Spanish. They chat briefly.][57]

Carlos Pereira of the House of Spice:

> Sure you are connected, you feel connected, not because you come to the Market and work at the House of Spice, it *is* [that], but it is people that make it more interesting. We get a bunch of people from all over … a lot of old customers. I get customers coming here for thirty years. They come to see me; you have to keep the relationship.[58]

Chapter Four

From Sites of Memory to Memoryscape: Wisdom Sits in Place[1]

Sensing a place – is a form of cultural activity.
                    – Keith H. Basso, *Wisdom Sits in Places*[2]

What binds Kensington Market together is that all of its sites are vehicles of memories, capsules of experience, the material expressions of past times and events. These sites stand out not simply because of their architectural significance[3] but also because, after more than a century of inevitable changes, they continue to work as *loci* of meaning for individuals and communities. Space and time reinforce each other and anchor our individual and collective experiences. With regard to preservation, Kevin Lynch emphasizes a sense of local continuity over the saving of particular *things*;[4] in the context at hand, the preservation issues in Kensington Market are ultimately emotional and familial. The Market has become a uniquely sensuous experience, one that blends sights, sounds, smells, and flavours, both daily and fleeting, often pleasant, sometimes not. Yi-Fu Tuan captures this well: "A person in the process of time invests bits of his emotional life in his home, and beyond the home in his neighborhood."[5] Kent Ryden writes that such places "weave themselves inextricably into the fabric of daily experience."[6] René Dubos concurs: "I remember the mood of places better than their precise features because places evoke for me life situations rather than geographical sites."[7]

In his study of environmental history, William Cronon argues that "to shift from chronicle to narrative, a tale of environmental change must be structured."[8] He suggests that "what distinguishes stories from other forms of discourse is that they describe an action that begins, continues over a well-defined period of time, and finally draws to a definite close, with consequences that become meaningful because of their placement within the narrative ... Narrative is a peculiarly human way of organizing reality, and this has important implications for the way we approach the history of environmental change."[9] Clare Cooper Marcus (in Altman and Low, *Place Attachments*) incorporates "place" aspects into her examination of narratives, in terms of environmental memories.[10] She argues that "the subtle but powerful blending of place, object, and feeling is so complex, so personal, that it is unlikely that the process will ever be fully explained ... In the sense that memory of place is a universal human experience, we are all alike; in the sense that a person's memories are unique, accessible, and meaningful only to that person, specific memories embedded in place cannot be fully experienced by anyone else."[11] While recognizing this "peculiarly human way of organizing reality," I choose to focus on the universal aspects that compress those personal experiences into community memories in Kensington Market.

The Market's residents have, without thinking to, transformed their ordinary built environment into a storied place. For my interviewees, it was memories and places as *loci memoriae* that generated the most discussion. Settling in Kensington Market had been a challenge for them, as it would have been in any foreign culture. Robert Harney reminds us that "in our celebration of multiculturalism we must not fail to recognize an immigrant's first years as years of constraint and to see that time as a crucible whereby his response to small but daily sights in his new country and his attachment to his country to origin."[12] In the Market, new immigrants overcame language and cultural barriers as they carved out a niche for their businesses.[13] They adjusted and adapted, survived and thrived. Most of them were hard-working, customer-oriented, and eager to get on with their lives. "Pioneers always try to use the past as a template by which to cut the future."[14] The first generation of immigrants in Kensington Market set out to plant roots in a parcel of land and merge it with their identity. They are still tenacious; their personal struggles, and those of the community as a whole, are now etched on Kensington Market, where multiple layers of memories are always visible. Those memories permeate their present-day experiences; place-centred narratives then vividly portray those experiences. Thus one site of memory tells a single story; several sites, synthesized, tell a collective story. Working together, different components and dimensions of those narratives provide perspectives and add emotional depth to Kensington Market.

Connection – with Kensington Market, with Families, with Communities

The sense of "feeling connected" sustains the soul of Kensington Market. Nostalgia – from the Greek *nosos*, "return to native land," and *algos*, "suffering or grief" – saturates Kensington Market. David Lowenthal is quite correct that "if the past is a foreign country, nostalgia has made it the foreign country with the healthiest tourist trade of all."[15] Even when the physical structures that support places are gone, those places remain strangely haunted. The third generation of the Hyman family recalled how people remembered Ben Zion Hyman and his bookstore long after it was gone: "In the last few years of Ben Zion's life, when he went to the nearest synagogue on the Sabbath, people still recognized him and talked about how the bookstore on Spadina was part of their life … They showed him the greeting cards that he made, or the books purchased from the store."

When a place changes its physical location – as with United Bakers – nostalgia spurs people to recall and revisit, as if to transport themselves back to it. Ruthie, the third generation co-owner of United Bakers, described how, after it moved, the restaurant continued to be a meeting place:

> The garment industry was a very vibrant industry, and today when every-thing is manufactured offshore, that is not the case. Everything was manu-factured on Spadina Avenue. The needle trade was a very very important business on Spadina, and there were a lot of Jewish merchants who owned factories, manufactured their garments there, sold to all of the stores. So yes, United Bakers was a hub, because it was a centre not just for gar-ment industry, but really, the Bay street lawyers would come over and have lunch at United, the physicians at Mount Sinai hospital would come over and have lunch at United. The Toronto Jewish Congress at the time was over on Beverley street, and they used to walked along D'Arcy street, across Spadina Avenue, and they had lunch at United. The fur traders union was all in the area, and the Labor Lyceum was just north of us. So everybody that worked in the area would come and have lunch at United. It was a real meeting spot. The same as it is today. [Ruthie emphasizes this continuity with a rising tone, even without my questioning]
>
>   What makes it so unique [today] is that every day somebody will come in, and share stories with us, of their memories, of having their first meal in Canada at United Bakers on Spadina, knowing my father, knowing

my grandfather and grandmother. Even today, a lot of the older population are passing away, but there are still, not many, but a handful of them that remember ... Particularly the older population, people that know my grandfather, who grew up on Spadina Avenue, who are now in their seventies. Even Mel Lastman, who grew up in Kensington Market, comes here regularly. Sure, Mel comes here all the time ... You know, they grew up in Kensington, and they grew up with United Bakers as part of their life. And they continue to eat here, and they continue to share stories, and it is a really wonderful feeling to have so many people come here to feel the connection to our family, to feel the connection to our lives.

In a later interview, I was fortunate to have Philip, Ruthie's brother and co-owner of United Bakers, sitting across the table with us. Philip provided another perspective on "feeling connected":

In Jewish religion, in Hebrew, we have a very famous saying: "All Israelis are responsible for each other." There is no independence in the Jewish religion. The worst thing to say is that I am not part of a group. The group is above all individuals. Our grandfather came from where the religion was much stronger, so he would feel strongly for all of us, and a necessity for being connected. Our father was raised in Canada, and he had a big heart. He was a wonderful man, and he was very aware of his responsibility to take care of what he could do for the community. He enjoyed it, really enjoyed it!

Both Ruthie and I were also raised in Canada, and we take a more cosmopolitan rather than a parochial view of life. Both of us take a huge pride in the fact we have this opportunity, this business opportunity and also this social opportunity and this family opportunity. We also say we are sitting in a great scene, watching a parade marching past. But we are not just sitting and watching the parade, Ruthie is always handing something to the people in the parade. We also try to make them feel we are connected. Connection is essential in the Jewish belief.

Ruthie added:

My father, Herman, spent a lot of time at the Ontario Jewish Archives. To honour his memory when he passed away, we had a plaque put up there. [The plaque says] "A Jew is not a Jew unless he is a member of a community." Community is a very important aspect of Judaism. Our grandfather was a centre of the Jewish community, because every new immigrant that came to this country was looking for a connection to somebody. United Bakers was the spot that he could come to and to find that connection. My grandfather and grandmother would come to facilitate that connection. [You know,] they would be able to say to them, "Oh, there is somebody from your *shtetl* that comes in here as well." Or "somebody you can connect to." They were the centre of the community.

The relationship between community and place is indeed a powerful one: each reinforces the identity of the other, and the streetscape is very much an expression of communal beliefs and values and of interpersonal relations. Relph summarizes these mutual bonds of people and place: "People are their place and a place is its people, and however readily these may be separated in conceptual terms, in experience they are not easily differentiated."[16] In Kensington Market, this connection has become the "Kensington spirit." Tom poignantly described that attachment:

In 1980 and 1981 I took over the store ... In my whole life, I paid attention to people, human beings. They were important to me. The new technology I do not bother. There are people who helped me with the techy part. I am interested in the personal contact, because that is how it was done. Fifty years ago when we started our business, the owner knew all his customers. I think that every single customer should be recognized. If you have customers supporting you over the years, they deserve some kind of recognition. The only way we can recognize their shopping habits, their shopping pattern, if they come to my store, is to try to give them a discount, and make them feel important, and that is what I don't see in today's world – the customer is not made important. Profit is important to stay in business, but it is not always important. Fifty years or forty years ago, when you came down to Kensington Market, the owner worked everyday. He knew what the customers wanted, and he carried the products the customers needed. And he had that personal love and that attachment to his customers.

When asked whether this attachment had changed over the years, he said it had:

Yes, it has changed ... There are lots of businesses in the world that we do not know about, businesses that are small, tribal businesses. They grow certain foods and vegetables near their area, then take it to their marketplace and sell it to their community. They play a very important role in the community by growing those vegetables and those fruits. They have done the businesses for hundreds of hundreds of years the same way: they grow it, cultivate it, and they take it to the marketplace. It is not a big business, but it is a very important business that they do. I feel that small businesses that do business with the public should go back to the old method: know their customers, know their products, watch their expenses, and like I said, reward your customers for coming and shopping with you. That is how I learned forty or fifty years ago in Kensington Market, and that's how it was. You build the relationship with your customers, and you build a bond. Their needs become your needs, and their problems become your problems.

Continuity: An Evolving and Cross-Generational Process

The relationship between Kensington Market and its people reflects a tenacious sense of continuity. Here family businesses have deep roots, and this fosters a cross-generational process in which living actors continue to make the place so as to generate a living and public history (Figure 4.1). Authenticity grows out of a profound awareness of places for what they are – which is, outcomes of human intentions. In the Market, this continuity is evident in how sites are interpreted, how businesses are run, and how faith and cultural values are inherited. Rabbi Levy of the Kiev synagogue observed:

A lot of congregants were involved in building it, carpenters, bricklayers, and such. A few months ago we had a Bar Mitzvah. This boy's great-grandfather was the carpenter involved in building the dome, so to have his great-grandson stand underneath the dome, reading from Torah on the day of his Bar Mitzvah, is very neat in terms of multigenerational connections.

Similarly, Ruthie commented:

As Philip said, my father carried on that business in very much the same way, very much a centre of the community, and today, too, we carry it on the same way. Today I say to you, if you come here, not only for a delicious meal, but want to know if your sister-in-law is here, and just ask ... [Laughing, Philip interjects, "Just ask her!"] Yes, I would tell you.

Continuity flourishes *because of* changes over time, not in spite of

Figure 4.1. Hebrew calendar for children at United Bakers. A nice touch with Jewish roots. Courtesy: Philip Ladovsky.

them. This is because people yearn to anchor their lives. Tom expressed his attitude towards the changing landscape:

> [The Market] was very Jewish, and now the Asian influx is very positive. Also the African influx ... [Now you have] a different life in the Market. Now we have more eateries, clothing stores ... The Market is evolving. We do not have many butcher shops, not many chicken stores. Now the market has got a different feel. You have more young people coming to the Market. I hope they will appreciate what this Market stands for, and what has gone into the Market. How many lives were built up there, and how hard it was for a lot of people to start here forty, fifty, sixty, seventy, or eighty years ago.

It was not easy ... All the small business [people], they took their lifesav-ings, they took a risk. They were wonderful people. We had bakeries, dair-ies. They were very proud of what they were able to produce or make – that was very important. That piece of bread is the best bread in the city. If you told them otherwise, they would take their coats off, put the apron on. The owner, it did not matter how successful he was, he would prove to you that was good bread. You do not have owners nowadays who know how to bake, or how to make cheese. The butcher was owned by a butcher – he knew how to cut that piece of meat. They loved what they were doing.

When stores change owners, the new owners try to carry on the tradi-tions of their predecessors. Max and Son, Meat Market, at 206 Baldwin Street, is an example (Figure 4.2). It opened in 1930 as a poultry shop, in the days of the Jewish Market. Max and Solly Stern owned it until Sep-tember 2009, just as I was beginning my field research. Peter Sanagan, a

Figure 4.2. Max and Son.

young and energetic chef, took over and renovated the store. The newly published books on meat culture, elegantly arranged on a shelf, are a breath of fresh air for the old store. At the same time, the historic photographs displayed on the walls serve as reminders of the store's roots. Peter has genuine respect for the store's past, and he enjoys chatting with its long-time customers.

Many old stores in the Market have continued selling similar products over the years, accommodating particular cultural groups. They are carrying on both a cultural tradition and a family history.

Survivance: **Culturally Rooted**

I earlier introduced the concept of *survivance* – the idea of cultural maintenance through the preservation of the home culture, including a whole bundle of habits, customs, tendencies, learnings, memories, political and religious affiliations, codes of conduct, and educational practices. *Survivance* finds expression in how owners decorate their stores, the kinds of products they sell, the particular groups they serve, and the languages in which they communicate. Kensington Market enjoys what Robert Harney observes, "all that is potentially rich in neighborhood terms – multi-racial harmony, commitment to quality, private initiative and an integration of employment and residential life for many who are there."[17] Sidonio Freitas of Perola:

> I have tried to model the store after some of the stores that I visited in Mexico when I was younger. I do the same here. I think it works, because a lot of people tell me that when they come here, they feel they have come to Mexico. We just have our ways with people, and keep our customers friends ... Keep what my parents are doing, their way of running the store. It is also about not minding hard work, long hours.[18]

Yvonne Grant of Caribbean Corner:

> [We have been] selling the similar kinds of products, and we have all kinds of customers. We have black people from the Caribbean, and we have people from Africa, South America, and some Asian customers.[19]

Most stores accommodate particular groups, just as in the Market's early years, when different immigrant groups created their own ethnic and cultural enclaves. Today, people feel at home at those stores, where they can speak their native tongue with the owners and other customers. As a result, their memories are culturally informed, as Tom Mihalik of Tom's Place suggests:

> I hang out here on Kensington, Baldwin, College, or Spadina. My friends live in the area, and we went to each other's stores. The market was in my blood, and it still is. I have fabulous memories of this place. My friends, my neighbours, they all love me, because they knew me since I was a kid. I knew my life was my business ... Because of the family influence, I knew I had to help my family. Yes, I still go back to Hungary. But I am living my dream. Canada allows me to live my dream: Canada has given me so much that I can never repay it. They give me dignity and respect. They allow me to be me, and the vehicle to have my own business, to be able to operate my business. I could never have done this in Hungary. I stay, and I do not want to move.[20]

Figure 4.3. Interior of Perola Supermarket.

Figure 4.4. A little corner of the Caribbean. Yvonne told me that over the years, she imported the same yams from Jamaica, where she was born.

Chapter Five

A Sense of Time and a Sense of Place:
The Past Is Not a Foreign Country[1]

For generations, a beautiful river of time has flowed through Kensington Market. We need to listen to place-centred narratives with an ear carefully tuned to culture. As Kevin Lynch perceptively writes, "a sense of the stream of time is more valuable and more poignant and engaging than a formal knowledge of a remote period."[2] Places conjoin time and space. When we approach places in terms of the intimately human, we find that urban landscape preservation holds great social potential and is a source of creativity.

When we link sites together into a narrative, a living memoryscape becomes visible to us. That memoryscape can provide a vitally important perspective for planners and their practices; it can also expose what is invisible in "official" interpretations of Kensington Market. A sense of place comes to the surface when space takes on three dimensions – that is, when it acquires *depth:* "Part of this depth is physical. Knowledge of place is grounded in those aspects of the environment which we appreciate through the senses and through movement: colour, texture, slope, quality of light, the feel of wind, the sounds and scents carried by that wind."[3]

I started this study with a map of Kensington Market of the sort that planners use, a map that is bland, dimensionless, stripped of human stories. It is a planners' map. The poet Elizabeth Bishop identifies the limitations inherent in this kind of map: "It compresses the landscape's ambiguity into an arbitrary and simplified flatness – it is all surface, lacking depth. This lack of depth takes in the human dimension as well; just as the map freezes the landscape in stasis so that waves no longer lap at beach and land no longer pulls at water."[4] Local residents follow a different kind of map, one with different mental textures. Bishop injects her poetic creativity into the map; her poetry enacts the perennial urge to connect with streetscape in ways both imaginative and humane.

Angèle Debeau's musical tour of old Toronto in *Old Toronto Klezmer Suite* serves as a sonic illustration of this point.[5] "Places served humankind as durable symbols of distant events and as indispensable aids for remembering and imagining them," writes Basso in *Wisdom Sits in Places*. "If place-making is a way of constructing the past, a venerable means of doing human history, it is also a way of constructing social traditions and, in the process, personal and social identities."[6] Maps, when based on human narratives, show "the spirit of places, and they preserve[] the memory of how people [feel] about places." This is the kind of map we as planners need to make and use when planning for preservation. When we value collective memory, urban streetscapes take on a deeply human scale. Planners who embrace that scale are no longer merely bureaucrats, officials, communicators, or facilitators; they are able to listen, collect, and analyse human details and thus develop more nuanced positions.

Many scholars have explored the values-based approach to managing cultural resources. Some view heritage as an important means to define and protect both individual and group identity;[7] others draw on heritage as a resource for comprehending social values.[8] Randall Mason summarizes the different kinds of values attached to heritage sites. "Sociocultural values are at the traditional core of conservation – values attached to an object, building, or place because it holds meanings for people or social groups due to its age, beauty, artistry, or association with a significant person or [otherwise] contributes to processes of cultural affiliation."[9] Historical, cultural/symbolic, social, spiritual/ religious, and aesthetic values all belong to this category. By contrast, economic valuing is "one of the most powerful ways in which society identifies, assesses, and decides on the relative value of things, which includes use (or market) value, [or] nouse (or nonmarket) value."[10] Values-centred preservation strategies applaud culture for its dynamism and try to include a greater range of stakeholders when arriving at a holistic understanding of place;[11] but such strategies also assume that full knowledge of those values will generate the best decisions. Unfortunately, that assumption is faulty. *Value* is a loaded term: it refers to the price of something in relation to some other thing; in other words, it is always relative. Left out of that equation is space for beauty, justice, freedom, eternity – qualities embedded in the historic environment that cannot be grasped in terms of values.

Mason understands that memory culture (a term coined by Andreas Huyssen[12]) "demands a different sort of preservation practice,"[13] but he does not fully explain *how*. The spirit of urban places is supported and sustained by intangible things, such as memories. But how can those things be measured? Indeed, can intangibles actually exist? Jean-Luc Nancy poses similar questions: "What can be said today without price? What can be said outside of any evaluation? Or, if you desire the object of an absolute value, without a comparative term? What can it be if we can on longer designate, determine, what used to be called a 'Good Sovereign'?"[14] In the field of preservation, authenticity has long been a cherished goal, but when we come up against intangible heritage, we do not yet have a clear benchmark. However fragile and resilient, the immaterial outlives individuals' lifespans, expands across generations, continually interacts with changing communities; ultimately, the immaterial is contingent on culture. To interpret intangible aspects of the tangible environment, we need to demystify historical authenticity.[15]

A culturally sensitive narrative approach, with its qualitative and critical spirit, focuses on the intangible, the immeasurable, the priceless. This approach works best in communities whose social history is still being made. Many of the issues now confronting Kensington Market reflect today's urban preservation dilemmas. Based on my direct experience with that neighbourhood, I suggest the following six steps:

1. The gathering of background information, including quantitative and qualitative data on demographics, geography, economic development, architectural styles, material culture, and, most important, *social history*.
2. Interpretive analysis, which would involve examining earlier preservation policies, with a focus on the role of the public, the results of *public participation*, and pivotal events.
3. Cultural immersion and field investigation, which would be largely *ethnographic*. This could be carried out on different scales based on the resources available.
4. The building of narratives, by identifying key interview respondents and conducting oral history interviews, preferably in the field.
5. The reframing of preservation policies, by distilling themes from different narratives and tying them together. The frame of reference would be local perspectives. The results would be validated through public meetings with stakeholders.

6. The implementation of new preservation policies. Communications with stakeholders (especially residents) would be kept open through public debates.

Those steps form an organic process, and can be carried out at different scales. The material representations often stand as triggers of collective memories and symbols, thus revealing the deep psychological and cultural trajectory of a group, so step 1 of CSNA emphasizes the social practices and logics behind the chosen site. This was what I found missing in existing studies about Kensington Market: there was plenty of rich, descriptive news-type work, but I did not see much written from insider perspectives. If it is either impractical or in many cases inappropriate to transfer from outsiders to denizens of the place, professional knowledge should, at least, contribute to the practical situations. At issue here is not only the role of professionals, but also professional authority and effectiveness.

Step 2 focuses on preservation policy analysis. This type of policy analysis presupposes that we live in a social world characterized by multiple possible interpretations. It assumes that knowledge is acquired through interpretation, so the interpretive approach is less an argument contesting the nature of reality than one about the human possibility of knowing the world around us and the character of that knowledge.[16] Situated within the interpretive tradition, this approach emphasizes the social dimensions of reality construction and focuses on the meanings of policies, on the values, feelings, or beliefs they express, and on the process by which those meanings are communicated to and read by various audiences.

Humanistic philosophy aligns itself with a communicative turn in urban planning.[17] Judith Innes argues for the paradigm status of communicative planning, stating that planning is more than anything else an interactive, communicative activity.[18] Systematic analysis and logical argument are only part of what planners do – indeed, a tiny part. John Forester applies Habermas's critical communications theory to planning practice to clarify how that practice works as *communicative action* and how broader political and economic forces may thwart *or* foster democratic planning.[19] Often when knowledge clashes with values, planners deploy stakeholder-based, consensus-building processes.[20] Elisabeth Hamin has proposed and applied an "interpretive planning model," which focuses on the following: (a) deconstruction and interpretation of planning documents; (b) the stories told by planners about their work; and (c) the role in the process for storytelling or *communication in planning*.[21]

Table 5.1. Steps in Interpretive Policy Analysis vs Kensington Market Project

Steps in Interpretive Policy Analysis Model	Steps in Kensington Market Project
1. Identify the artefacts (language, objects, acts) that are significant carriers of meaning for a given policy issue, as perceived by actors and interpretive communities.	a. Written documents: 1957 Market Plan, 1962 Market study, 1966–9 Urban Renewal Program and detailed study of Kensington, 1960s Spadina Expressway project b. Built environment: altered or demolished as a result – how to tell a policy story?[23]
2. Identify communities of meaning/interpretation/speech/ practice that are relevant to the policy issue being analysed	a. Professionals (planners and city officials) b. Kensington Area Residents Association (KARA)[24] c. Kensington Urban Renewal Committee (KURC) d. Kensington Market Businessmen's Association (KMBA) e. Spadina Businessmen's Association (SBA) f. Local residents: property owners, tenants, and business owners
3. Identify the "discourses": the specific meanings being communicated through specific artefacts and what they entail (in thoughts, speech, and acts)	Not applicable
4. Identify the points of conflict and their conceptual sources (affective, cognitive, and/or moral) that reflect different interpretations by different communities	a. Problems, including traffic congestion, lack of laneways, parking, and servicing problems → the professional vs the public b. Special identity or neighbourhood character → understanding of urban renewal → different cultural assumptions underlie what constitutes "identity" or "character" c. Power and representation d. Cultural and language issues
5. Interventions/actions 5a. Show implications of different meanings/interpretations for policy formulation and/or action 5b. Show that differences reflect different way of seeing 5c. Negotiate/mediate/intervene in some other form to bridge differences	Public participation → interpretation of the goal of participation can generate conflict: decentralization of decision making; redistribution of political or economic power; citizen groups developing their own planning and leadership processes Demolition vs preservation → insiders vs outsiders: Who owns the building/space? Whose memory, whose history?

Earlier, this book examined urban renewal planning for Kensington Market in the 1960s, a decade when urban redevelopment in Toronto confronted the general failure of modernist planning. It identified the pivotal events that led to changes in urban renewal policies, and it showed how failed attempts at urban renewal were in fact a *success* for Kensington Market, in that it resulted in the Market being preserved on its own terms, as a sort of public history lesson. More specifically, my analysis followed Dvora Yanow's steps towards an interpretive policy analysis model.[22] An interpretive community develops around a shared point of view with respect to a given policy issue. Such a community can be identified through documentary analysis, including City of Toronto Planning Board minutes, residential association minutes, city directories, and census records.

Steps 3 and 4 require a substantial amount of fieldwork. After all, oral history is a deeply "social practice connecting past and present, and at times, connecting narratives to action."[25] In terms of what Linda Shopes calls a "problem-centered approach,"[26] the primary concern for Kensington Market is the built environment – its public and community spaces, as well as its housing stock. The interpretive community takes its shape around the intersections of individual lives. This study focused on those with long-term associations with the area. However, for a fuller picture of transformed landscapes, outsiders and newcomers were also interviewed. The interview outline was based on Robert Harney's *Oral Testimony and Ethnic Studies*[27] and Petroff's *Oral Testimony and Community History: A Guide.*[28]

Thus, the interviewees were encouraged to describe their early lives and places of origin, their occupational and geographical mobility patterns, and their migration history and perspectives on immigration. According to Perry Blatz, interviewers should "encourage interviewees to speak as fully as they choose about their lives."[29] However, there are differences between life history interviews and oral histories. A life history is a multidisciplinary research method with roots in psychology, ethnography, and oral history. It clarifies individuals' life stories, shows how those stories represent a coherent whole, and highlights relations with other individuals' life stories as well as with the entire community. It often offers a linear version of personal history. Oral history, by contrast, records, preserves, and interprets historic information in a broader social and cultural context. It includes folklore, myths, songs, and stories passed down over generations. In the 1980s, when oral history and memory studies emerged almost simultaneously, the two approaches framed their research questions differently. Yet when the inquiry moves beyond individual and family boundaries into the community, oral history becomes extremely valuable for analysing memories as they are made public. In the Kensington Market project, life history comprised only part of the interviews. I adopted the *Sample Life-Story Interview Questions* from the Centre for Oral History and Digital Storytelling at Concordia University. Those questions helped establish rapport between the interviewer and the informants. That said, the overarching theme of this project remains place and memory.

After the study sites were selected,[30] I researched the available documents, drawings, plans, and historic photographs for each. I also studied existing oral histories from a variety of sources.[31] Most of these had not been summarized, much less transcribed, so it was difficult to establish a proper context for interpreting them. However, I was able to find two more recent oral histories that offered fuller depictions, one of which combined biographical information with insights about the evolution of Kensington Market.[32] When analysing the secondary oral history data, I paid heed to the "gap between living through an experience and studying from the experience,"[33] especially in terms of the social context in which the interviews took place.

Ellen Scheinberg, then director of the Ontario Jewish Archives, suggested a few possible interviewees, most of whom had family attachments to the selected sites, such as Gurion and Ruth Hyman and Philip Ladovsky. For the Market, I started with the city records to identify the oldest stores or the persons who had resided there longest. While tracking down the interviewees, I immersed myself in Kensington Market for field investigation and participant observation. These ethnographic activities included taking building-by-building, street-by-street photographs, comparing them with historic photographs and cross-referencing them with city records; talking informally with store owners and visitors to identify possible interviewees; participating in the Sabbath service at the Kiev synagogue on Saturdays (from 9 a.m. to noon), and celebrating Kiddush with the congregants afterwards; visiting and eating at United Bakers; and so on.

I approached Kensington Market as a cultural landscape, or a *locus*, defined by Casey as "a place easily grasped by the memory."[34] D.W. Meinig wrote in *The Interpretation of Ordinary Landscapes* that

[such a viewer] begins by being at once comprehensive and naive: by encompassing all and accepting everything he sees as being of some interest. It is landscape as environment, embracing all that we live amidst, and thus it cultivates a sensitivity to details, to texture, color, all the nuances of visual relationships, and more, for environment engages all of our senses, the sounds and smells and ineffable feel of a place as well. Such a viewer attempts to penetrate common generalizations to appreciate the unique flavor of whatever he encounters.[35]

As I gathered sensory experiences, Kensington Market became my academic fascination. To develop a more accurate picture of the neighbourhood, I visited various sites at different times of day and on different days each week. From late May to late July 2009, I spent three days a week there, five hours on average each day.

In August 2009, I began conducting interviews. Then, using the snowball technique, I developed a second-round list of interviewees. For each place, I conducted three or four deep interviews; with some interviewees, I arranged follow-ups. Most often, I called the interviewees to briefly introduce myself and the project. Fortunately, all of them were quite willing to sit for interviews, so it was more challenging to accommodate different schedules than to find informants. With the exception of Hyman's Bookstore (now the Jewish Public Library), all the interviews took place in a home or a store, where I was able to observe while interviewing. The interviews thus were a wonderful opportunity to observe the daily life of the individual storeowners and the community as a whole.

The interview data were not transcribed verbatim, because much of the point of interviewing would have been lost. Oral history data are a *source* of history, not history, so tampering with its form or content would not make it more authentic or accurate, according to Robert Harney. So instead of transcribing the interviews verbatim, I used *Stories Matter,* an oral history database tool that allows for the archiving of digital video and audio materials and enables researchers to annotate, analyse, and evaluate oral history data.[36] I processed the field data between November 2009 and February 2010 while working as a visiting oral historian at the Center for Oral History and Digital Storytelling at Concordia University.

Not all of the interviewees are quoted in this book. I have restricted the number of quotes for the sake of deepening the narrative and presenting a fuller picture of each site I have chosen. For maximum validity and accuracy, I have used only the interviews I conducted and taped, though the relevant interviews listed in the previous sheet provided helpful information in organizing the themes.[37] Most of the interviewees from the Market spoke English as their second or third language, so they often made grammatical errors. To ensure the accuracy and also to better capture the tone, such as *how* things were described and *how* opinions were expressed, I have corrected errors only when clarity requires it.

Step 5 and 6 relate to future preservation policy-making. Though not fully carried out in Kensington Market project, I see this can become a blessing rather than a regret, if put in a broader context. Why? When the public cannot participate extensively, or when public voices have been excluded from policy-making, planners can at least document narratives for future use. As Kevin Lynch writes, "saving the past can be a way of learning for the future, just as people change themselves by learning something now that they may employ later."[38]

Having been trained as a planning scholar, I believe in authenticity and objectivity. Much of my educational and professional life has been dedicated to achieving both. Yet I have come to realize the gap between the skills and techniques I learned in academia and use in planning practices *and* the voices of users of the places I try to preserve and plan. The public history behind the bricks and mortar in specific places has not been sufficiently addressed. To address this problem, we, as professionals, need to learn to identify emotionally with the places we are studying and cultivate a shared humanity with those whose lives overlap with that of their community.

In the end, what do I want to share with my fellow urban planners? This book about Kensington Market describes how CSNA works. Central to this approach are (a) building a critical case, (b) understanding the local, "insider" culture, and (c) building and analysing place-centred narratives.

Conducted within the interpretive and critical traditions, CNSA essentially aims to build critical cases, from which anticipations for that particular and other similar situations can be created. Robert Yin defines the case study as "an empirical inquiry that ... investigates a contemporary phenomenon within its real-life context, especially when ... the boundaries between phenomenon and context are not clearly evident."[39] According to Yin, case studies consider distinct situations in which there are many more variables of interest than data points. Thus they rely on multiple sources of evidence, and they benefit from theoretical propositions when it comes to data collection and analysis. So the strength of a case study lies in its ability to deal with a full variety of evidence – documents, artefacts, interviews, and observations – beyond what might be available in a conventional historical study.

Bent Flyvbjerg has examined common misunderstandings about case study research and has reached these conclusions: concrete, context-dependent knowledge is more valuable than predictive theories and universals; the fieldwork involved in most in-depth case studies is valuable because "the field" is a "powerful disciplinary force: assertive, demanding, even coercive";[40] and summarizing case studies is often difficult, especially as concerns processes, so often it is not desirable to generalize from them. Good studies should be read as narratives.[41]

Flyvbjerg's findings are highly relevant to CSNA for three reasons.[42] First, the theory of collective memory and urban space is contextually and culturally dependent. CSNA is meant to apply a narrative approach in a culturally diverse setting, so it needs to assemble the greatest possible amount of information on a given problem or phenomenon. For that reason, a representative case or a random sample would not be the most appropriate strategy.[43]

Second, in terms of both understanding and action, it is often more important to clarify the deeper causes of a given problem than to describe the symptoms of the problem and how often they occur. Michael Barzelay argues that "a single case can yield several kinds of results, each of which should be valued by anyone who seeks to improve collective problem solving."[44] In the study at hand, "collective problem solving" relates to how to work with a local community that is trying to preserve its neighbourhood. The value of an in-depth case study lies not in the facts it gathers or the theories it generates but in "the contextual and interpenetrating nature of forces."[45] To build a "critical case" here is to generate information that permits logical deductions of the type "if this is (not) valid for this case, then it applies to all (no) cases."[46]

Third, an in-depth analysis often involves narratives that reflect the complexities and contradictions of real life. Accordingly, narratives generated from fieldwork may be difficult or impossible to summarize into neat scientific formulae, general propositions, or theories. A case study is oriented towards cultural understanding of the "insiders" – their perspectives, emotions, memories, and senses of place. To follow Clifford Geertz, a case study involves *thick description*, with multiple and contradictory levels of local meanings from the field. Detailed observations may not always yield a meaningful understanding of a situation. Only by wading through multiple complex layers of local interpretations and by sorting through what Geertz calls the "structure of signification" or "web of significance" can one arrive at a more comprehensive and insightful cultural portrait.[47]

To ensure the validity of CSNA, I suggest we test the resulting analysis for the trustworthiness of the interpretation rather than for its truth, as suggested by Reissman,[48] for the truth of an interpretation is bounded by empirical realities and scholarly consensus.[49] Yin's approach to case studies[50] would strengthen their validity.

1. Constructing Validity
   - Use multiple sources of evidence →documentary analysis, oral history interviewing, observation, material cultural analysis (data collection and analysis).
   - Establish chain of evidence →identify sources of interpretive gap in article II to guide fieldwork for article III, site selections, follow research protocol, and track database (data collection and analysis)
   - Have key informants review draft case study report → have key informants review either the whole draft or the relevant portion of the draft (data analysis)
2. Internal Validity
   - Explanation building →interpretive analysis of preservation policies
3. External Validity
   - Replication logic →build a critical case (data analysis)
4. Reliability
   - Use case study protocol → oral history interviewing guide (data collection)
   - Develop case study database → keep four separate field notes: 1. Short notes made at the time; 2. Expanded notes made immediately after the interview; 3. A field journal to record new ideas occurring at each stage of research; 4. A provisional running record of analysis and interpretation.[51] Along with taped interviews, those notes are cross-referenced to ensure the reliability of field data.

I hope this book has shown that the more tightly collective memory is integrated with communicative planning through narratives or storytelling, the greater the likelihood that urban landscapes will be identified with communities' senses of place and that preservation will succeed. This would make it possible to address emotionally compelling issues embedded in an urban built environment without compromising academic or professional rigour. Kevin Lynch wrote more than forty years ago that "a new profession may be developing: the manager of an ongoing environment (the spatial and temporal pattern of things and human actions), whose profession it is to help users to change it in ways that fit their purposes."[52] Urban landscapes should be interpreted and preserved as public history, and the most efficient way to accomplish this seems deceptively simple and matter-of-fact: local residents should be encouraged to record memories of their neighbourhoods. Our task, then, is to help the public better understand the environment in which they reside, to broaden their individual perspectives into collective ones, and, ultimately, to preserve a past to which they are emotionally committed.

Notes

Preface

1 Tung, *Preserving the World's Great Cities*, 11.
2 Jan Morris writes in the Foreword to Kluckner, *Toronto the Way It Was:* "Half the world, it often seems, has settled in Toronto, whether by choice or by circumstance; and most of contemporary humanity's aspirations, I think, whether they are expressed in supermarket abundance, political urbanity or a mere yearning for easy-going, mind-your-own-business, evenings-before-the-TV lack of passion, have chosen to settle in this city too."
3 Prior to site selection, I conducted an extensive review of the general literature on Kensington Market and of the local media coverage. This review included an architectural inventory of the buildings along the principal streets in the Market (Architectural Conservancy of Ontario); existing oral history data, mainly from the Ontario Jewish Archives (OJA) and the Multicultural Historical Society of Ontario (MHSO); immigrant settlement history in general and Jewish history in particular; and a number of unpublished manuscripts (City of Toronto Archives, Archives of Ontario). Buildings within the boundaries of the designated districts have been documented by the Historic Sites and Monuments of Canada (HSMBC).

1. Memory and History: Urban Landscapes as Public History

1 For a more detailed discussion on collective memory and public history, see Li and Hamin, "Preservation."
2 Glassberg, *Sense of History*, 207.
3 Erll, *Memory in Culture*, 15.

4 Erll, *Memory in Culture,* 97.
5 Glassberg, *Sense of History.*
6 Erll, *Memory in Culture,* 21.
7 Halbwachs and Coser, *On Collective Memory,* 188.
8 Sandercock, "Towards Cosmopolis," 402. See also Sandercock, "Out of the Closet."
9 Hayden, *The Power of Place,* 46.
10 Boyer, *The City of Collective Memory,* 21.
11 Lynch, *What Time Is This Place?,* 43, 88.
12 Boym, *The Future of Nostalgia,* xv.
13 Assmann and Czaplicka, "Collective Memory and Cultural Identity."
14 Erll, *Memory in Culture,* 27.
15 Harney and MHSO, *Gathering Place.*
16 Erll, *Memory in Culture,* 28–9.
17 Alanen and Melnick, *Preserving Cultural Landscapes in America,* 94–111.
18 This does not have to be the extreme versions such as historic traumas; rather, it can refer to different interpretations of the same historic events. I contend that, if we can demonstrate the extreme, the rest will become easy to argue. So we relax the assumption, because the challenges facing preservation planners are different. Competing values must be balanced *locally.*
19 Williams, in *Culture and Society,* explores this pattern in terms of the following dichotomies: the middle classes and less powerful groups; males and females; heterosexuals and those who are not; majority lifestyles and diverse, multicultural ones; cities and the countryside; high culture – including architecture – and low culture (which encompasses history, archaeology, and cultural landscapes); "settler" cultures and values and Indigenous ones in post-colonial settings; and in general, "dominant" culture and "residual" or "emergent" culture. Instead of broadly integrating culture, I focus on history and its more intangible cultural implications.
20 Kare Umemoto suggests that respecting and navigating cultural protocols and social relationships is one challenge in participatory planning. She defines protocols as codes of etiquette, which can take on greater importance in more formal meetings or gatherings. Also, these codes cover a range of behaviours, such how one addresses others, how one defers to a mutually acknowledged social hierarchy, whether one attends sacred or social events, what symbolic offerings one makes, the norms of exchange and reciprocity, and even how discussions are begun. Umemoto, "Walking in Another's Shoes," 24.
21 Rigby, *Citizen Participation,* 70.

22 Field, Meyer, and Swanson, *Imagining the City*, 9.
23 Forester, *The Deliberative Practitioner*.
24 Lynd, "Oral History from Below."
25 Shopes, "Oral History."
26 Hayden, "Placemaking"; Hayden, *The Power of Place*.
27 Lerner, *Why History Matters*, 118.
28 Relph, *Place and Placelessness*, 64.
29 Mason, "Theoretical and Practical Arguments," 21.
30 The Historic Sites and Monuments Board of Canada (HSMBC), founded
    in 1919, advises the Minister of the Environment about the national
    significance of places, persons, and events in Canada's history. Almost
    80 per cent of the nominations it considers are made by the public. When
    making a positive recommendation to the minister, the board offers advice
    on a commemorative plaque. For more about the HSMBC, visit http://
    www.pc.gc.ca/eng/clmhc-hsmbc/comm-board.aspx.
31 Letter from Dr Carlos Teixeira to Dr Michel Audy, Executive Secretary,
    HSMBC, 24 March 2003. Courtesy of HSMBC.
32 White, "Kensington History Honoured."
33 Steinbeck, *Travels with Charley*, 208.

2. Kensington Market – an Urban Neighbourhood, a Cultural Metaphor

1 Cochrane and Pietropaolo, *Kensington*.
2 Taylor, *The Villages Within*.
3 No census data are available for the period prior to 1800.
4 Gagan, *The Denison Family*.
5 Bellevue Avenue was named after the first house in the area, Belle Vue,
    the home of George Taylor Denison (1783–1853). George was born in
    England and came to Upper Canada at the age of eight. In December 1806
    he married Esther Borden Lippincott, who owned three thousand acres
    in Richmond Hill. He built Belle Vue at the northeast corner of Bellevue
    Avenue at Denison Square. This Georgian home was surrounded by his
    farmlands, orchards, woods, and a ravine. Denison accumulated much of
    his wealth through marriage (four times). At his death in 1853, he owned
    of 556 acres of Toronto and was one of its wealthiest citizens. Belle Vue was
    demolished in 1890. Wise and Gould, *Toronto Street Names*.
6 Rigby, *Citizen Participation*, 26.
7 There was very little separation of land uses in the city by 1834.
8 Rigby, *Citizen Participation*, 26.

96   Notes to pages 13–16

9 Waldron, "Kensington Market."

10 John Graves Simcoe, first lieutenant governor of Upper Canada, who envisioned that the original "park lots" in the Kensington Market–College Street area would be developed as English-style country estates; Peter Russell, appointed receiver general of the province in 1792; John Denison, a friend of Russell's from Yorkshire; Dr William Warren Baldwin and his family, Robert, Phoebe, Sullivan, and Willcocks; and George Taylor Denison, all named streets in the area after family members. Baldwin Street, for example, is named after William Warren Baldwin (1775–1844), an influential figure in early York. Denison, Bellevue, Lippincott, Borden, and Major are only a few of the names that have survived until today. See Wise and Gould, *Toronto Street Names*.

11 The area has always attracted immigrants. "In 1890s and early 1900s, the city's Italian population began moving out of the Ward (bounded by Queen, Young, College and University, to the neighborhood around College and Grace street). By 1916, Toronto's second Little Italy boasted its own Catholic church, St. Agnes, on Grace street, a Methodist meeting place, a steamship agency, a real estate office, as well as several small grocery stores." Myrvold, *Historical Walking Tour*, 6.

12 Kluckner, *Toronto the Way It Was*, 142.

13 Harney and Troper suggest that immigrant patterns were influenced by commercial development and the routing of streetcars, among other things. For example, housing in the Ward was torn down in order to build hospitals, and sewer lines were extended west along College Street. All of this drew Italians westward towards the College–Manning area. Harney and Troper, *Immigrants*.

14 Harney suggests two possible reasons for this surge: first, many British began to move to better housing above College Street, as well as to new suburbs like Mount Pleasant and Leaside, following the expanding streetcar system; and second, Toronto's original Jewish neighbourhood was being demolished after 1916 to build Toronto General Hospital and Sick Children's Hospital and to expand commercial development along York Street. Harney, "Kensington Market Area."

15 Rigby, *Citizen Participation*, 27.

16 Refer to City of Toronto Planning Board, *Kensington Recommended Official Plan*, 1978.

17 In a "real" street market, most of the vendors' stands do not share commercial or social relations with the adjoining properties, and those who have stalls in the market bring goods in or out every day. Kensington Market has the appearance of a street market because the shops lining the

street sell goods mainly from stands and other structures that extend out onto the street allowance and sidewalk from the fronts of the buildings, and also because much of the trade is conducted on the street.

18 "Recognized the Neighborhood's Old World Charm," *Toronto Star,* 18 July 1925.

19 Rigby, *Citizen Participation.*

20 Directory of the City of Toronto, 1961.

21 Lemon, *Toronto Since 1918,* 193.

22 My interview with Tom Mihalik at 190 Baldwin Street, 16 January 2010.

23 See Teixeira and Da Rosa. *The Portuguese in Canada,* 22.

24 Teixeira and Da Rosa, *The Portuguese in Canada.*

25 Kensington Market Census Tract 38, College to Dundas and Spadina to Bathurst Streets, Toronto Reference Library.

26 Kensington Market Census Tract 38.

27 Harney and MHSO, *Toronto: Canada's New Cosmopolis,* 1.

28 Those include the expansion of Toronto Western Hospital; the expansion of the University of Toronto for a married students' residence; and the expansion of the Provincial Institutes of Trades (which would become George Brown Community College). Also, the Toronto Board of Education was proposing to build a new school. Cochrane and Pietropaolo, *Kensington,* 89.

29 Toronto Planning Board, 1967.

30 Rose and University of Toronto, *Citizen Participation,* ii.

31 Rose and University of Toronto, *Citizen Participation,* 21.

32 Rose and University of Toronto, *Citizen Participation.*

33 Rose and University of Toronto, *Citizen Participation.*

34 Toronto Planning Board, June 1966, 5.

35 City of Toronto Planning Board, 1973.

36 Historic districts are geographically defined areas that create a special sense of time and place through buildings, structures, and open spaces modified by human use; these are united by past events and uses and/or aesthetically, by architecture and plan. See Canada, HSMB, *Criteria.*

37 Waldron, "Kensington Market," 4–5.

38 HSMBC, "Historic Districts and the Historic Sites and Monuments Board of Canada," 2000, 1.

39 Waldron, "Kensington Market," 14.

40 Segovia's at 216 Augusta, and the Paradise Bay Fish Shack up the street at 257, are typical examples of warm colours being painted onto the ubiquitous Toronto red brick. See Waldron, "Kensington Market."

41 Waldron, "Kensington Market."

42 Speisman, *The Jews of Toronto,* 72.

43 Speisman, *The Jews of Toronto*.
44 The interior of a Jewish immigrant home. See Harney and Troper, *Immigrants*, 33.
45 Bureau of Municipal Research (Toronto), 1918;Harney and Troper, *Immigrants*, 34.
46 Riis, *How the Other Half Lives*.
47 See Bauman, "A Saga of Renewal."
48 Tuan, *Topophilia*, 210.
49 Keller, *The Urban Neighborhood*, 87–8.
50 Keller, *The Urban Neighborhood*, 108.
51 The built environment refers in the broadest sense to any physical alteration of the natural environment, from a hearth to a city, through construction by humans. It generally includes built forms, spaces, and landmarks or sites. Lawrence and Low, "The Built Environment."
52 King, "The Social Production," 1. For a more comprehensive literature review on the social production of the built form, a wonderful start is provided by Lawrence and Low, "The Built Environment."
53 Sauer and Leighly, *Land and Life*, 343.
54 Lane, "Franco-American Folk Traditions," 60.
55 See M. Giguere, "Introduction."
56 Myrvold, *Historical Walking Tour*, 15.

3. Collective Memory and Kensington Market

1 Donegan and A Space, *Spadina Avenue*, 18. See also Hiebert, "Fashion District/Spadina," PhD diss., University of Toronto.
2 Aristotle, *The Physics*, 201a20–1.
3 Aristotle, *The Physics*, 449a9.
4 Yates, *The Art of Memory*, 6.
5 Yates, *The Art of Memory*, 117–27, 387–8.
6 Casey, *Remembering*, 210.
7 Casey, *Remembering*, 213.
8 Casey, *Remembering*, 189.
9 Basso, *Wisdom Sits in Places*, 7.
10 Jones, "An Ecology of Emotion," 205.
11 Anderson and Smith, "Editorial."
12 Opp and Walsh, "Introduction," 14.
13 *Genius loci* is a Latin term roughly meaning "spirit of place." In the context of a historic district, integrity refers to the degree to which a site conveys its national significance according to the attributes identified (i.e., location,

setting, design, materials, use, and association). In the case of Kensington Market, there are four aspects to consider: the conveyance of the place's historic value through its physical features; the existence of a sense of place (that tangible and intangible quality that gives a place special meaning); the ongoing function of the site; and the continuation of a dynamic evolutionary quality to the site. See Waldron, "Kensington Market."

14 Liebman, "Three Toronto Synagogues," 10.

15 Heschel, *The Sabbath*, 96–7.

16 A guideline for assessing the needs of the individual was prepared by the Conservative Organization of Synagogues. That guideline included items such as the following: a house of worship, study and assembly; a Hebrew school for children; a wholesome environment for teenagers; adult social contact – men's clubs, sisterhoods, young adult groups; and a place to foster a sense of belonging. Liebman, "Three Toronto Synagogues," 13.

17 Speisman, *The Jews of Toronto*.

18 Pinkus, "History of the Kiever."

19 Pinkus, "History of the Kiever." It seems a pleasant coincidence that Toronto's name is derived from the Huron word for "meeting place" and that the word "synagogue" comes from the Greek *synagein*, "to bring together" (i.e., meeting place). More generally, the purpose of the synagogue is threefold: to house Jewish congregational worship, study, and community meetings.

20 Heschel, *God in Search of Man*, 254.

21 Heschel, *Man Is Not Alone*, 241–2.

22 Tuan, *Topophilia*, 106.

23 E.V. Walter contrasts place and space: modern space is universal and abstract, whereas a place is concrete and particular. People do not experience abstract space; they experience *places*. A place is seen, heard, smelled, imagined, loved, hated, feared, revered, enjoyed, or avoided. Abstract space is infinite; in modern thinking it means a framework of possibilities. A place is immediate, concrete, particular, bounded, finite, unique. See Walter, *Placeways*.

24 Graham, "An Examination," 22.

25 Built by the oldest Jewish congregation in Toronto, Holy Blossom features twin towers and a dome with an elaborate facade.

26 Ezekiel 11:16 (NIV). This is a key verse in Ezekiel, as the symbol of God's presence among his people.

27 This sort of boxlike mass is often seen in buildings of the mid-twentieth century. Sometimes in older, nineteenth-century buildings, the roof is especially low in slope and plain in profile, with no towers, a compact hall,

and a rectangular or square floor plan – as simple as can be. See Ontario Heritage Trust.

28 The relevant verse is from Nehemiah 8:4: "Ezar the scribe stood on a high wooden platform built for the occasion" (NIV). That occasion was to read the law from the pulpit.

29 Psalm 130:1: "Out of the depth I cry to you, O, Lord" (NIV).

30 Krinsky, *Synagogues of Europe*, 21.

31 Yi-FuTuan, who has analysed architectural space and awareness, observes that the built environment clarifies social roles and relations. Tuan, *Space and Place.*

32 Canadian Jewish Congress, Central Region, Minutes of the Archives Committee, 27 February 1974.

33 Ontario's Ministry of Citizenship and Culture had granted the committee $115,000, but Martin Mendelow, the project's architect, estimated the restoration costs as $400,000. The remaining $285,000 would have to come from donations. In June 1975 the committee organized a cantorial concert on Denison Square as well as an exhibit on the history of the Kiever in the social hall in the basement of the *shul*. Also, Sol Edell and Albert Latner tried to raise funds by contacting institutions, companies, and individuals for donations into the early 1980s. The foundation sold honorary memberships and provided limited-edition copies of a watercolour of the Kiev made by Martin Mendelow as an incentive for donations of more than $1,000. Various individuals and companies contributed by providing construction services and supplies. Toronto First Synagogues project.

34 Toronto's First Synagogues project.

35 In Hebrew, *makom* means "place" or "space." It is also an ancient rabbinic name for God, signifying God's omnipresence, the felt sense of God's immanence in the world and our lives. Under the leadership of Rabbi Aaron Levy, Makom has injected fresh blood into the historic Kiev. According to the organization's Makom Mission Statement, "We are a Jewish community rooted in downtown Toronto, both in the present and historically. Downtown is not just our geography, but our ethos. The spaces we inhabit as a community (The Kiever Synagogue, Kensington Market, Bellevue Park, Queens Park, and more) inform our identity, just as we influence our spaces through our activities in them."

36 My interview with Rabbi Aaron Levy, 26 and 29 October 2009.

37 See Goldstein and Shulman, *Voices from the Heart*, 90–1.

38 My interview with Gurion Hyman, 13 October 2009.

39 According to Gurion Hyman, his father had a gift for languages: "Always comfortable with different languages, speaking Yiddish, Hebrew, and Russian, and by studying French and German, he was able to make contact

with a Parisian company that was selling patterns for making dresses."
40 This cute story comes from my interview with Ruth Hyman, 13 October 2009.
41 My interview with Gurion Hyman, 13 October 2009.
42 My interview with Gurion and Ruth Hyman, 13 October 2009.
43 Rabinovitch, "Of Cabbage Borscht and Kreplach," 48.
44 Rabinovitch, "Of Cabbage Borscht and Kreplach," 49.
45 Ruthie Ladovsky has been an extraordinary help in my understanding of Jewish dairy practices.
46 Donegan and A Space, *Spadina Avenue*, 24.
47 My interview with Ruthie Ladovsky, on 8 December 2009.
48 Yerushalmi, *Zakhor*, 44–5.
49 The Market here is used in a narrow sense: it refers to the market area bounded by Kensington Avenue, Baldwin Street, and Augusta Avenue.
50 Murray (Edward) McLauchlan, Canadian folksinger and songwriter. His early style was characterized by a twangy toughness that corresponded with his view of, and from, the underclass. His later work grew more personal in tone. Although his style has changed over time, his songwriting has remained faithful to the folk tradition and aims at a working-class audience. "Down by the Henry Moore"(1975) reflects this working-class ethos. It does not, however, portray the poverty of Kensington Market, especially during the first half of the twentieth century.
51 My interview with David Borg, 14 January 2010.
52 My interview with Tom Mihalik, 16 January 2010.
53 My interview with Sidonio Freitas, 26 January 2010.
54 My interview with Carlos Pereira, 21 January 2010.
55 My interview with Yvonne Grant, 21 January 2010.
56 My interview with Yvonne Grant, 21 January 2010.
57 My interview with Sidonio Freitas on 26 January 2010.
58 My interview with Carlos Pereira, 21 January 2010.

4. From Sites of Memory to Memoryscape: Wisdom Sits in Place

1 Refer to Basso, *Wisdom Sits in Places*.
2 Basso, *Wisdom Sits in Places*, 143.
3 The Kiev was designated partly for the wrong reason, I believe.
4 Lynch, *What Time Is This Place?*, 235.
5 Tuan, *Topophilia*, 99.
6 Ryden, *Mapping the Invisible Landscape*, 39.
7 Dubos, *A God Within*, 87.
8 Cronon, "A Place for Stories," 1367.
9 Cronon, "A Place for Stories," 1367.

10 Altman and Low, *Place Attachment*, 88.
11 Altman and Low, *Place Attachment*, 111.
12 Harney and MHSO, *Toronto*, 10.
13 This is the case for almost all of the sites, even Hyman's bookstore: Fanny Hyman, Ben's hard-working wife, was an incredible businesswoman who helped him run the bookstore until she passed away in 1970(?). I did not start with those themes because written documents tell very little about the psychic world of such places. Similarities emerged from field observations and interviews. This is how I think the CSNA differs from other policy level narratives: planners have already had a preconceived idea and sometimes come to the table simply to hear what they expect to hear. The narratives are edited to serve the goal they want to achieve.
14 Stegner, *Wolf Willow*, 288.
15 Lowenthal, *The Past Is a Foreign Country*, 4.
16 Relph, *Place and Placelessness*, 34.
17 Harney and MHSO, *Toronto*, 19.
18 My interview with Sidonio Freitas, 26 January 2010.
19 My interview with Yvonne Grant, 21 January 2010.
20 My interview with Tom Mihalik, 16 January 2010.

5. A Sense of Time and a Sense of Place: The Past Is Not a Foreign Country

1 "The past is a foreign country" was first used in L.P. Hartley's *The Go-Between*: "The past is a foreign country: they do things differently there" (1). More relevant to the subject of this research, however, is David Lowenthal's well-known book, *The Past Is a Foreign Country*.
2 Lynch, *What Time Is This Place?*, 237.
3 Ryden, *Mapping the Invisible Landscape*, 38. For the term *memoryscape*, see Butler, "Memoryscape," 360.
4 Ryden, *Mapping the Invisible Landscape*, 21.
5 This loving tribute to the great Canadian composer Srul Irving Glick serves as a musical tour of Toronto's old Jewish community, guided by the violinist Angèle Dubeau, who has performed the suite many times. (Dubeau and La Pieta perform Glick on the CD *Violons du Monde*; Analekta AN 2 8721). Other music featured was "Agadah" from Glick's *Suite Hebraique* #4 for alto saxophone and piano, performed by Paul Brodie and Valerie Tryon. "The Old Toronto Klezmer Suite," with Angele Debeau and Steven Speisman, CBC Radio, *Fresh Air*, 16 December 2002.
6 Basso, *Wisdom Sits in Places*, 7.

7 Mason, *Assessing Values in Conservation Planning*, in Fairclough et al., *The Heritage Reader*, 104; Russell, "Heritage, Identities, and Roots."

8 Okamura, "A Consideration of Heritage Values."

9 Mason, "Assessing Values in Conservation Planning," 104.

10 Waldron, "Kensington Market."

11 Mason, "Theoretical and Practical Arguments," 21–48.

12 Huyssen, *Present Pasts*.

13 Mason, "Theoretical and Practical Arguments," 28.

14 Nancy, "The Insufficiency of 'Values,'" 439.

15 Many works on intangible heritage have emerged over the last decade, especially since 2003, when the UN Convention for the Safeguarding of the Intangible Cultural Heritage established an international effort to understand and preserve intangible heritage around the world. Smith and Akagawa's *Intangible Heritage* offers across-section of ideas and practices associated with the concept. See also Morgan et al., "From National to Local."

16 Yanow, *Conducting Interpretive Policy Analysis*, 5–7.

17 Planning researchers adopt different terms, such as "argumentative," "linguistic," or "rhetorical turn," to describe essentially the same collective efforts to provide alternative perspectives on modernist rational concepts of planning. James Throgmorton suggests that this is closely related to Habermas's effort to reconstruct the dialectic of the Enlightenment in terms of communicative reason; to Gadamer's call for dialogue oriented towards a fusion of horizons; to Rorty's pragmatic conception of rationality as civility; to Lyotard's reference to the breakdown of all grand narratives; to Foucault's interpretation of professionalized discursive formation as will to power; to Derrida's claim that scientific texts can be deconstructed as works of literature; to Geertz's emphasis on the locality and contextuality of knowledge; and to recent explorations of the rhetorical nature of scientific inquiry and professional practice. See Throgmorton, *Planning as Persuasive Storytelling*, 29n. I would argue that they emphasize the humane dimension of planning practice, which has long been ignored. My later analysis of storytelling in planning will support this contention. See also Fischer and Forester, *The Argumentative Turn*; Fischler, *Communicative Planning Theory*; Forester, *The Deliberative Practitioner*; Healey, 1992, 1999; Innes, "Planning Theory's Emerging Paradigm"; Throgmorton, Mandelbaum, and Garcia, "On the Virtues of Skillful Meandering."

18 Innes, "Planning Theory's Emerging Paradigm."

19 Forester, "Critical Theory and Planning Practice."

20 Forester, *Planning in the Face of Power*.

21 Hamin, *Mojave Lands*, 176.

22 Yanow, *Conducting Interpretive Policy Analysis,* 21–2.
23 Dvora Yanow broadens the policy interpretations from traditional literal texts to include spaces created or built in response to policy mandates. She argues that such buildings may be viewed as telling policy stories. Yanow, "Built Space as Story." A growing body of work has begun to deal with the narrative, rhetorical, and textual character of political theory and policy analysis.
24 The Kensington Area Residents Association (KARA) was founded in 1967 to coordinate the activities of residents who were trying to save the community and individual homes. These residents were opposed to any sweeping demolition of existing housing, but they also saw the need for community renewal. They called for a community-oriented approach so that any renewal would maintain the neighbourhood's identity and historical streetscape. With KARA's help, an Urban Renewal Committee composed of residents, businesspeople, and the ward alderman was formed to advise city council on matters affecting the Kensington area. Wallace, "Planning Amidst Adversity."
25 Hamilton and Shopes, "Introduction," in *Oral History and Public Memories,* viii.
26 Shopes, "Beyond Trivia and Nostalgia," 151–8.
27 Harney and MHSO, *Oral History,* 1978.
28 Petroff, *Oral Testimony.*
29 Blatz, "Craftsmanship and Flexibility," 22.
30 The study was approved by the Human Subject Institutional Review Board (IRB) and Human Research Protection Office (HRPO) at the University of Massachusetts–Amherst on 13 January 2010.
31 They include the Ontario Jewish Archives, the MHSO, the City of Toronto Archives, Archives of Ontario, Library and Archives Canada, the Toronto Reference Library, the Lillian H. Smith Library (near Kensington), the St Stephen's House Kensington Alive Exhibit, and Murmur/Kensington, among others.
32 One comes from the Ontario Jewish Archives. Mel Lastman was interviewed by Ellen Scheinberg, the director of those archives, in 2006. Ellen suggested a few possible interviewees, most of whom had family connections to the chosen sites, such as the Hyman family and the current owners of the United Bakers.
33 Grele, "On Using Oral-History Collections," 573.
34 Casey, *Remembering,* 202.
35 Meinig, *The Interpretation,* 45.
36 For a detailed introduction to *Stories Matter,* refer to the training manual

from the Centre for Oral History and Digital Storytelling, Concordia University, Montreal.

37 All the interview data were analysed with *Stories Matter* (Phase I).

38 Lynch, *What Time Is This Place?*, 43.

39 Yin, *Applications of Case Study Research*, 12.

40 Geertz, *The Interpretation of Cultures*, 119.

41 See Flyvbjerg, "Five Misunderstandings."

42 For predictive theory, universals, and scientism, the study of human affairs is thus at an eternal beginning. In essence, we have only specific cases and context-dependent knowledge.

Misunderstanding 1: General, theoretical (context-independent) knowledge is more valuable than concrete, practical (context-dependent) knowledge. This can be revised as follows: Predictive theories and universals cannot be found in the study of human affairs. *Reformulation*: Concrete, context-dependent knowledge is, therefore, more valuable than the futile search for predictive theories and universals.

Misunderstanding 2: One cannot generalize on the basis of individual cases; therefore, case studies cannot contribute to scientific development. The balanced view of the role of the case study in attempting to generalize by testing hypotheses has been formulated by Eckstein (1975): "Comparative and case studies are alternative means to the end of testing theories, choices between which must be governed largely by arbitrary or practical, rather than logical, considerations ... It is impossible to take seriously the position that case studies are suspect because they are problem-prone and that comparative studies deserve the benefit of doubt because they are problem-free" (pp. 116, 131); see also Barzelay, "The Single Case Study."

Misunderstanding 3: The case study is most useful for generating hypotheses – that is, during the first stage research; other methods are more suitable for hypothesis testing and theory building.

Misunderstanding 4: The case study is biased towards verification – that is, it tends to confirm the researcher's preconceptions. Geertz, in *The Interpretation of Cultures*, said about the fieldwork involved in most in-depth case studies that the field itself is a "powerful disciplinary force: assertive, demanding, even coercive" (119). Like any such force, it can be underestimated, but it cannot be evaded. "It is too insistent for that." Case studies are no more biased towards the researcher's preconceptions than any other method of inquiry. On the contrary, experience indicates that case studies are more biased *against* preconceptions.

Misunderstanding 5: It is often difficult to develop general propositions and theories on the basis of specific case studies. *Reformulation*: It is correct that summarizing case studies is often difficult, especially as regards processes. This is less correct as regards case outcomes. But the problems in summarizing case studies are often due more to the properties of the reality being studied than to the use of case studies as a research method. Often it is not desirable to summarize and generalize case studies. Good studies should be read as narratives in their own right.

43 This is because the typical or average case is often not the richest in information. Atypical or extreme cases often reveal more information because they activate more actors and more basic mechanisms in the situation being studied. See "Strategies for the Selection of Samples and Cases (table)," in Flyvbjerg, "Five Misunderstandings."

44 Barzelay, "The Single Case Study."

45 Peattie, "Communities and Interests," 260.

46 Flyvbjerg, "Five Misunderstandings," 230.

47 Webs of significance: "Our day-to-day lives are replete with layers upon layers of meaning, woven together in complex symbolic system[s]. All human action is suspended in webs of significance that can be apprehended only by grasping the specific local interpretations engaged in by the natives themselves. It is like trying to read a manuscript – foreign, faded, full of ellipses, incoherencies, suspicious emendations, and tendentious commentaries, but written not in conventionalized graphs of sound but transient examples of shaped behavior." Geertz, *The Interpretation of Cultures*, 43.

48 Riessman, *Narrative Analysis*, 1993.

49 Kirk and Miller, *Reliability and Validity*.

50 Yin, *Applications of Case Study Research*, 34.

51 I borrow this method of keeping separate field notes from Spradley, *The Ethnographic Interview*. The last point comes from Kirk and Miller, *Reliability and Validity*.

52 Lynch, *What Time Is This Place?*, 239.

Bibliography

Below are the some of the key planning documents and records relating to Kensington Market.

KMBS (Kensington Market Business Association). 1973–80."Kensington Market Businessmen's Association." City of Toronto Archives.

Board, C.o.T.P. 1955–62, 1963–68. "Urban Renewal Study, Kensington." City of Toronto Archives.

Board, C.o.T.P. 1966. "An Application for Federal and Provincial Approval and Assistance in the Preparation of Kensington Urban Renewal Scheme." Archives of Ontario.

Board, C.o.T.P. June1966. "An Application for Federal and Provincial Approval and Assistance in the Preparation of Kensington Urban Renewal Scheme."

Board, C.o.T.P. May1, 1969. "Kensington Urban Renewal Scheme."

KARA (TKARsA). "Re The Establishment of An Urban Renewal Committee for the Kensington Area. Scheme 29, Toronto – Kensington General." 10 June 1968.

J.F. Brown, S. "Urban Renewal Section (8 August 1969). Memo: Kensington Urban Renewal Committee – Report and Recommendations." 3 July 1969.

Toronto, H.A.o.1967. "Kensington Area Redevelopment." City of Toronto Archives.

Primary Sources

Alanen, Arnold, and Robert Melnick, eds. *Preserving Cultural Landscapes in America*. Baltimore.: Johns Hopkins University Press, .

Altman, Irwin, and SethaLow, eds. *Place Attachment*. New York: Plenum Press, http://dx.doi.org/10.1007/978-1-4684-8753-4.

Anderson, Kay, and Susan Smith. "Editorial: Emotional geographies." *Transactions of the Institute of British Geographers* 26, no. 1 (2001): 7–10. http://dx.doi.org/10.1111/1475-5661.00002.

Aristotle. *The Physics*. Translated by P.H. Wicksteed and F.M.Cornford. Cambridge, MA: Harvard University Press, 1960.

Assmann, Jan, and John Czaplicka.1995. "Collective Memory and Cultural Identity." *New German Critique* 65 (1995): 125–33. http://dx.doi.org/10.2307/488538.

Barzelay, Michael. "The Single Case Study as Intellectually Ambitious Inquiry." *Journal of Public Administration Research and Theory* 3 (1993): 305–18.

Basso, Keith. *Wisdom Sits in Places: Landscape and Language among the Western Apache*. Albuquerque: University of New Mexico Press, 1996.

Bauman, John. "A Saga of Renewal in a Maine City: Exploring the Fate of Portland's Bayside District." *Journal of Planning History* 5, no. 4 (2006): 329–54. http://dx.doi.org/10.1177/1538513206294203.

Blatz, Perry. "Craftsmanship and Flexibility in Oral History: A Pluralistic Approach to Methodology and Theory." *Public Historian* 12, no. 4 (1990): 7–22. http://dx.doi.org/10.2307/3378782.

Boyer, M. Christine. *The City of Collective Memory: Its Historical Imagery and Architectural Entertainments*. Cambridge, MA: MIT Press, 1994.

Boym, Svetlana. *The Future of Nostalgia*. New York: Basic Books, 2001.

Bureau of Municipal Research. *What Is "The Ward" Going to Do with Toronto? A Report on Undesirable Living Conditions in One Section of the City of Toronto, "The Ward," CConditions Which Are Spreading Rapidly to Other Districts*. Toronto: 1918.

Butler, Toby. 2007. "Memoryscape: How Audio Walks Can Deepen Our Sense of Place by Integrating Art, Oral History, and Cultural Geography." *Geography Compass* 1, no. 3 (2007): 360–72. http://dx.doi.org/10.1111/j.1749-8198.2007.00017.x.

Campbell, Susan, and Scott Fainstein.2003. *Readings in Planning Theory*. Malden: Blackwell.

Canada. HSMB (Historic Sites and Monuments Board). *Criteria, General Guidelines, and Specific Guidelines for Evaluating Subjects of Potential National Historic Significance*. Ottawa: 2008.

Casey, Edward S. *Remembering: A Phenomenological Study*. Bloomington: Indiana University Press, 1987.

Cochrane, Jean, and Vincenzo Pietropaolo. *Kensington*. Richmond Hill: Boston Mills Press, 2000.

Cronon, William. "A Place for Stories – Nature, History, and Narrative." *Journal of American History* 78, no. 4 (1992): 1347–76. http://dx.doi.org/10.2307/2079346.

Davidson, Joyce, Liz Bondi, and Mick Smith, eds. 2005. *Emotional Geographies*. Aldershot and Burlington: Ashgate, 2005.

Donegan, Rosemary, and A Space (Art gallery). *Spadina Avenue*. Vancouver: Douglas & McIntyre, 1985.

Dubos, Rene. *A God Within*. New York: Scribner, 1972.

Erll, Astrid. *Memory in Culture*. New York: Palgrave Macmillan, 2011.

Fairclough, Graham, Rodney Harrison, John Schofield, and John Jameson, Jr, eds. *The Heritage Reader*. New York and London: Routledge, 2008.

Field, Sean, Renate Meyer, and Felicity Swanson, eds. *Imagining the City: Memories and Cultures in Cape Town*. Cape Town: HSRC Press, 2007.

Fischer, Frank, and John Forester. *The Argumentative Turn in Policy Analysis and Planning*. Durham: Duke University Press, 1993. http://dx.doi.org/10.1215/9780822381815.

Fischler, Raphaël. "Communicative Planning Theory: A Foucauldian Assessment." *Journal of Planning Education and Research* 19, no. 4 (2000): 358–68. http://dx.doi.org/10.1177/0739456X0001900405.

Flyvbjerg, Bent. "Five Misunderstandings about Case-Study Research." *Qualitative Inquiry* 12 (2006): 219–45.

Forester, John. "Critical Theory and Planning Practice." *Journal of the American Planning Association* 46, no. 3 (1980): 275–86.

———. *Planning in the Face of Power*. Berkeley: University of California Press, 1989.

———. *The Deliberative Practitioner: Encouraging Participatory Planning Processes*. Cambridge, MA: MIT Press, 1999.

Frisch, Michael H.1990. *A Shared Authority: Essays on the Craft and Meaning of Oral and Public History*. Albany: SUNY Press, 1990.

Gagan, David Paul. 1973. *The Denison Family of Toronto*. Toronto: University of Toronto Press, 1973.

Geertz, Clifford. *The Interpretation of Cultures: Selected Essays*. New York: Basic Books, 1973.

Giguere, M. "Introduction." In Brigette Lane, *Franco-American Folk Traditions and Popular Culture in a Former Milltown*. New York: Garland, 1990.

Glassberg, David. *Sense of History: The Place of the Past in American Life*. Amherst: University of Massachusetts Press, 2001.

Goldstein, Bonnie, and Jaclyn Shulman, eds. *Voices from the Heart: A Community Celebrates 50 Years of Israel*. Toronto: McClelland & Stewart, 1998.

Graham, Sharon. "An Examination of Toronto Synagogue Architecture, 1897–1937." *Journal of the Society for the Study of Architecture in Canada* 30 (2001): 15–24.

Grele, Ronald J.1987. "On Using Oral-History Collections – an Introduction." *Journal of American History* 74 (2): 570–8. http://dx.doi.org/10.2307/1900139.

Halbwachs, Maurice, and Lewis A. Coser. *On Collective Memory*. Chicago: University of Chicago Press, 1992.

Hamin, Elisabeth M. *Mojave Lands: Interpretive Planning and the National Preserve*. Baltimore: Johns Hopkins University Press, 2003.

Hamilton, Paula, and Linda Shopes. *Oral History and Public Memories*. Philadelphia: Temple University Press, 2008.

Harney, R.F., and MHSO (Multicultural History Society of Ontario). *Gathering Place: Peoples and Neighbourhoods of Toronto, 1834–1945*. Toronto: 1985.

———. *Oral Testimony and Ethnic Studies*. Toronto: 1978.

———. *Toronto: Canada's New Cosmopolis*. Toronto: 1981.

Harney, Robert F., and Harold Troper. *Immigrants: A Portrait of the Urban Experience, 1890–1930*. Toronto: Van Nostrand, 1975.

Harney, Stephen. "Kensington Market Area: An Environmental Studies Project" (unpublished ms). 1976.

Hartley, L.P. *The Go-Between*. London: Hamish Hamilton, 1953.

Hayden, Dolores. "Placemaking, Preservation, and Urban History." *Journal of Architectural Education* 41, no. 3 (1988): 45–51. http://dx.doi.org/10.1080/10 464883.1988.10758490.

———. *The Power of Place: Urban Landscapes as Public History*. Cambridge, MA: MIT Press, 1995.

Healey, Patsy. "Institutionalist Analysis, Communicative Planning, and Shaping Places." *Journal of Planning Education and Research* 19, no. 2 (Winter 1999): 111–21.

———. "Planning through Debate: The Communicative Turn in Planning Theory." *Town Planning Review* 63, no. 2 (April 1992): 143–62.

Heschel, Abraham Joshua. *God in Search of Man: A Philosophy of Judaism*. New York: Farrar, Straus and Giroux, 1976.

———. *Man Is Not Alone: A Philosophy of Religion*. New York: Jewish Publication Society of America, 1951.

———. *The Sabbath: Its Meaning for Modern Man*. New York: Farrar, Straus and Giroux, 1951.

Hiebert, Daniel. "Fashion district/Spadina," part of PhD dissertation, University of Toronto.

HSMBC, "Historic Districts and the Historic Sites and Monuments Board of Canada," 2000, 1.

Hudson, Edna, and Architectural Conservancy of Ontario. Toronto Region Branch. *Bellevue Avenue: An Architectural and Social Study*. Toronto: 1993.

Huyssen, Andreas. *Present Pasts: Urban Palimpsests and the Politics of Memory*. Stanford: Stanford University Press, 2003.

Innes, Judith E. "Planning Theory's Emerging Paradigm: Communicative Action and Interactive Practice." *Journal of Planning Education and Research* 14, no. 3 (1995): 183–9. http://dx.doi.org/10.1177/073945 6X9501400307.

Jackson, John Brinckerhoff. *Discovering the Vernacular Landscape*. New Haven: Yale University Press, 1984.

Jones, Owain. "An Ecology of Emotion, Memory, Self and Landscape." In *Emotional Geographies*. Edited by Joyce Davidson, Liz Bondi, and Mick Smith. Aldershot and Burlington: Ashgate, 2005.

Keller, Suzanne. *The Urban Neighborhood: A Sociological Perspective*. New York: Random House, 1968.

King, A.D. "The Social Production of Building Form – Theory and Research." *Environment and Planning. D, Society & Space* 2, no. 4 (1984): 429–46. http://dx.doi.org/10.1068/d020429.

Kirk, Jerome, and Mark L. Miller. *Reliability and Validity in Qualitative Research*. Beverly Hills: Sage, 1986.

Kluckner, Michael. *Toronto the Way It Was*. Toronto: Whitecap Books, 1988.

Krinsky, Carol Herselle. *Synagogues of Europe: Architecture, History, Meaning*. Cambridge, MA: MIT Press, 1985.

Lane, Brigette. *Franco-American Folk Traditions and Popular Culture in a Former Milltown*. New York: Garland, 1990.

Lawrence, Denise L., and Setha M.Low. "The Built Environment and Spatial Form." *Annual Review of Anthropology* 19, no. 1 (1990): 453–505. http://dx.doi.org/10.1146/annurev.an.19.100190.002321.

Lemon, J.T. *Toronto Since 1918: An Illustrated History*. Toronto: James Lorimer, 2002.

Lerner, Gerda. *Why History Matters: Life and Thought*. New York: Oxford University Press, 1997.

Levitt, Sheldon, Lynn Milstone, and Sidney Tenenbaum. *Treasures of a People: The Synagogues of Canada*. Toronto: Lester &OrpenDennys, 1985.

Li, Na. 2010."Preserving Urban Landscapes as Public History: The Chinese Context." *Public Historian* 32, no. 4 (2010): 51–61. http://dx.doi.org/10.1525/tph.2010.32.4.51.

Li, Na, and Elisabeth M. Hamin. "Preservation." In *The Oxford Handbook of Urban Planning*. Edited by Rachel Weber and Randall Crane. New York and London: Oxford University Press, 2012.

Liebman, G. "Three Toronto Synagogues Which Became One" (1980). Unpublished article. Ontario Jewish Archives.

Lowenthal, David. *The Past Is a Foreign Country*. Cambridge and New York: Cambridge University Press, 1985.

Lynch, Kevin. *What Time Is This Place?* Cambridge: MIT Press, 1972.

Lynd, Staughton. "Oral History from Below." *Oral History Review* 21, no. 1 (1993): 1–8. http://dx.doi.org/10.1093/ohr/21.1.1.

Mason, Randall. "Assessing Values in Conservation Planning: Methodological Issues and Choices."In *The Heritage Reader.* Edited by Graham Fairclough, Rodney Harrison, John Schofield, and John Jameson, Jr.New York and London: Routledge, 2008.

———. "Theoretical and Practical Arguments for Values Centered Preservation." *CRM: The Journal of Heritage Stewardship* 3 (2006): 21–48.

Meinig, D.W., ed. *The Interpretation of Ordinary Landscapes: Geographical Essays.* New York: Oxford University Press, 1979.

Morgan, David W., Nancy I.M. Morgan, Brenda Barrett, and Suzanne Copping. "From National to Local: Intangible Values and the Decentralization of Heritage Management in the United States." in *Heritage Values in Contemporary Society.* Edited by George S. Smith, Phyllis Mauch Messenger, and Hilary A. Soderland. Walnut Creek: Left Coast Press, 2010.

Nancy, Jean-Luc. "The Insufficiency of 'Values' and the Necessity of 'Sense.'" *Journal for Cultural Research* 9, no. 4 (2005): 439. http://dx.doi.org/10.1080/14797580500252621.

Okamura, Katsuyuki. "A Consideration of Heritage Values in Contemporary Society." In *Heritage Values in Contemporary Society.* Edited by George S.Smith, Phyllis M.Messinger, and Hilary A.Soderland. 43–55.Walnut Creek: Left Coast Press, 2010.

Opp, James, and John Walsh. "Introduction: Local Acts of Placing and Remembering." In *Placing Memory and Remembering Place in Canada.* Vancouver: UBC Press, 2010.

Peattie, Lisa R. "Communities and Interests in Advocacy Planning." *Journal of the American Planning Association* 60, no. 2 (Spring 1994).

Petroff, Lillian. *Oral Testimony and Community History: A Guide.* Toronto: Multicultural History Society of Ontario, 2002.

Pinkus, David. "History of the Kiever." n.d. http://kievershul.tripod.com/history.html.

Rabinovitch, Lara. "Of Cabbage Borscht and Kreplach at United Bakers." *Edible Toronto* 7 (2009): 48–50.

Relph, Edward. *Place and Placelessness.* London: Pion, 1976.

Riessman, Catherine Kohler. *Narrative Analysis.* Newbury Park: Sage Publications, 1993.

Rigby, Douglas W. *Citizen Participation in Urban Renewal Planning: A Case Study of an Inner City Residents' Association.* University of Waterloo, Faculty of Environmental Studies, 1975.

Riis, Jacob A. 1971. *How the Other Half Lives*. New York: Dover, 2002.

Rose, Albert, and University of Toronto Centre for Urban and Community Studies. *Citizen Participation in Urban Renewal*. University of Toronto, 1974.

Russell, Ian. 2010. "Heritage, Identities, and Roots: A Critique of Arborescent Models of Heritage and Identity." In *Heritage Values in Contemporary Society*. Edited by George S. Smith, Phyllis M. Messinger, and Hilary A. Soderland.43–55. Walnut Creek: Left Coast Press, 2010.

Ryden, Kent C.1993. *Mapping the Invisible Landscape: Folklore, Writing, and the Sense of Place*. Iowa City: University of Iowa Press.

Sandercock, Leonie. "Out of the Closet: The Importance of Stories and Storytelling in Planning Practice." *Planning Theory and Practice* 4, no. 1 (2003): 11–28. http://dx.doi.org/10.1080/1464935032000057209.

———. "Towards Cosmopolis: Utopia as Construction Site." In Susan Campbell and Scott Fainstein, *Readings in Planning Theory*. 401–7. Malden: Blackwell, 2003.

Sauer, Carl O., and John Leighly. *Land and Life: A Selection from the Writings of Carl Ortwin Sauer*. Berkeley: University of California Press, 1963.

Sewell, John. *The Shape of the City: Toronto Struggles with Modern Planning*. Toronto: University of Toronto Press, 1993.

Shopes, Linda. "Beyond Trivia and Nostalgia: Collaborating in the Construction of a Local History." *International Journal of Oral History* 5, no. 3 (1984): 151–8.

———. "Oral History and the Study of Communities: Problems, Paradoxes, and Possibilities." *Journal of American History* 89, no. 2 (2002): 588–98. http://dx.doi.org/10.2307/3092177.

Smith, George S., Phyllis M. Messinger, and Hilary A. Soderland. *Heritage Values in Contemporary Society*. Walnut Creek.: Left Coast Press, 2010.

Smith, Laurajane, and NatsukoAkagawa. *Intangible heritage*. London: Routledge, 2009.

Speisman, Stephen A. *The Jews of Toronto: A History to 1937*. Toronto: McClelland & Stewart, 1979.

Spradley, James P. *The Ethnographic Interview*. New York: Holt, Rinehart and Winston, 1979.

Stegner, Wallace E. *Wolf Willow: A History, A Story, and a Memory of the Last Plains Frontier*. Lincoln: University of Nebraska Press, 1980.

Steinbeck, John. *Travels with Charley in Search of America*. New York: Penguin Books, 2002.

Taylor, Doug. *The Villages Within*. iUniverse, 2004.

Teixeira, Carlos, and Victor M.P.Da Rosa. *The Portuguese in Canada: Diasporic Challenges and Adjustment*. Toronto: University of Toronto Press, 2009.

Throgmorton, James A. *Planning as Persuasive Storytelling: The Rhetorical Construction of Chicago's Electric Future*. Chicago: University of Chicago Press, 1996.

Throgmorton, James A., Seymour Mandelbaum, and Margot Garcia. "On the Virtues of Skillful Meandering: Acting as a Skilled-Voice-in-the-Flow of Persuasive Argumentation." *Journal of the American Planning Association* 66, no. 4 (2000): 367–83. http://dx.doi.org/10.1080/01944360008976121.

Tuan, Yi-Fu. *Space and Place: The Perspective of Experience*. Minneapolis: University of Minnesota Press, 1977.

———. *Topophilia: A Study of Environmental Perception, Attitudes, and Values*. Englewood Cliffs: Prentice-Hall, 1974.

Tung, Anthony Max. *Preserving the World's Great Cities: The Destruction and Renewal of the Historic Metropolis*. New York: Clarkson Potter, 2001.

Umemoto, Kare. "Walking in Another's Shoes: Epistemological Challenges in Participatory Planning." *Journal of Planning Education and Research* 21, no. 1 (2001): 17–31. http://dx.doi.org/10.1177/0739456X0102100102.

Waldron, A.M. "Kensington Market, Toronto, Ontario." HSMBC (Historic Sites and Monuments Board of Canada), Submission Report 2005–30, 2005.

Wallace, Marcia. "Planning Amidst Adversity: The Challenges of Multiculturalism in Urban and Suburban Greater Toronto." PhD diss., University of Waterloo, 1999.

Walter, E.V. *Placeways: A Theory of the Human Environment*. Chapel Hill: University of North Carolina Press, 1988.

Whyte, Murray. "Kensington History Honoured: Market Designated National Historic Site although Residents Focus Mainly on Its Future." *Toronto Star*, 25 May 2008.

Williams, Raymond. *Culture and Society, 1780–1950*. Harmondsworth: Penguin Books, 1966.

Wise, Leonard, and Allan Gould. *Toronto Street Names: An Illustrated Guide to Their Origins*. Richmond Hill: Firefly Books, 2001.

Yanow, Dvora. "Built Space as Story: The Policy Stories That Buildings Tell." *Policy Studies Journal* 23, no. 3 (1995): 407–22. http://dx.doi.org/10.1111/j.1541-0072.1995.tb00520.x.

———. *Conducting Interpretive Policy Analysis*. Thousand Oaks: Sage , 2000. http://dx.doi.org/10.4135/9781412983747.

Yates, Frances A. *The Art of Memory*. Chicago: University of Chicago Press, 1966.

Yerushalmi, Yosef Hayim. *Zakhor: Jewish History and Jewish Memory*. Seattle: University of Washington Press, 1982.

Yin, Robert K. *Applications of Case Study Research*. Thousand Oaks: Sage, 2003.

Index

Page numbers followed by "f" refer to figures and followed by "t" refer to tables. They are also in italics. Page numbers followed by "n" refer to notes, and are followed by the note number.

activism, urban renewal priorities, 19–20
Afro-Caribbean Canadians: immigrant wave, 31; population, 17–18
Anderson, Kay, "Emotional Geographies," 38
Anglo-Saxon immigrants, 13, 15, 96n10
Aponte-Pares, Luis, 6
architecture: commercial vernacular, 23, 28, *29f*; glass storefront, 63, *65f*; Greek Cross in Sanci's, *58f*; immigration waves and, 25; Kiev Synagogue, 40–7, *41–8f*; memory hotspots, 4; narrow streets, eccentricities, 26–8, *27f*, 97n40; social history of built forms, 33, 98n52, 100n31, 104n23; studies of Market, xii; Victorian row houses, *26f*, 28, 31
Aristotle, *De Memoria et Reminiscentia*, 37

Asian/Chinese Canadians: immigrant wave, 31, 34, *35f*; Market population 1960s, 17–18
Assman, Aleida and Jan, cultural memory, 5
Augusta Avenue: architecture and historic designation, 26; canopies, awnings, and colours, 28, 31, 97n40; Casa Acoreana, *34f*; community, 60; ground floors converted to shops, 16; Jewish migration to, 15; map, *14f*; Portuguese immigration to, 17. *See also* House of Spice; Perola Supermarket
authenticity, 13, 38, 74, 82, 87, 88, 98n13

Bakers and Confectionary Workers International Union of America, 55
Baldwin Kosher Meat Market, 65
Baldwin Street: architecture and historic designation, 26, *27f*, *29f*;

Market, 16–18; studies of, xii;
survival/*survivance*, 19, 31, 33,
77–8
Immigration Act, 1962 amendments,
17
Innes, Judith, 83
insider/outsider perspectives, in
research focus, 10
institutional land use, 18
intangible heritage, 8–9, 82, 103n15
interpretive planning model, 83, *84t*,
85–6
interviews. *See* methodology
Italian Canadians, 96n11; first fruit
market by, 31, 58

Jacobs, Jane, 50
Jamaican Canadians: commercial
activity, 65–6, *79f*; Market
population, 17–18, 65
Jewish Canadians: community
sense, 37, 50, 56, 71–3; Eastern
European, 16, 17; intellectual
landscape, 50–4; move into Market
area, 15; move into the Ward,
13; peddlers, *15f*; synagogues,
32, 39–40, 99n16 (*see also* Kiev
Synagogue)
Jewish Market: continuity and
changes, *35f*, 62, 65, 75–6; origins
of, 15–16, 96n14; peddlers, *15f*, 32;
vernacular architecture of, 23, 28,
29f
Jewish Public Library, 54

Keller, Suzanne, 32
Kenney, Jason, 11
Kensington Area Residents
Association (KARA), 20, *21f*,
104n24

Kensington Avenue: community,
60; graffiti, *30f*; ground floors
converted to shops, 16; map, *14f*;
original houses (Victorian), *26f*, 31.
See also Caribbean Corner; Sanci's
Kensington Market:
commercialization of, 16;
continuity, 38–9, 74–7; historic
map (1884), *14f*; history of the
land of, 12–13; overview of case
study, 8–11 (*see also* methodology);
studies of, xii, 10, 84–7. *See also*
historical site designation of
Kensington Market; Jewish
Market
Kensington Market Businessmen's
Association (KMBA), *21f*
Kensington Revitalization Plan
(1980s), 22. *See also* urban planning
Kensington spirit, 73
Kensington Urban Renewal
Committee (KURC), *21f*
Kieltzer Society of Toronto, 55
Kiev Synagogue: architecture and
furnishings of, 40–7, *41–8f*, 99n27;
the *bimah*, 44–6, *46–7f*, 100n28;
continuity of community, 74; in
ethnographic study, 86; historical
site designation, 50; origins of,
39–42; Restoration Committee, 48,
50, 100n33; Women's Auxilary, 47,
47f. *See also* Jewish Canadians
King, Anthony D., 33
Kluckner, Michael, 13
Kwasniewski, David, 65

Labor Lyceum (on Spadina), 52,
53–4, 71
Ladovsky, Aaron and Sarah, 54–7,
72–3